# THIS BOOK BELONGS TO:

---

BY SHANNON FOSTER

WWW.THEREDHEADEDHOSTESS.COM

# THE BOOK OF MORMON

Fill this page full of quotes from modern day prophets that teach you something about the Book of Mormon.

# TABLE OF CONTENTS

1  THIS BOOK BELONGS TO...

2  QUOTES

3  TABLE OF CONTENTS

4  TABLE OF CONTENTS

5  READING CHART

6  HOW TO USE THIS BOOK

7  PAGE TITLES

8  PAGE TITLES

9  PAGE TITLES

10  PAGE TITLES

11  PAGE TITLES

12  1 NEPHI 1-4

13  1 NEPHI 5-8

14  WHAT IS THE HOUSE OF ISRAEL?

15  OLIVE TREE / WHAT IS A GENTILE?

16  1 NEPHI 9-12

17  1 NEPHI 13-16

18  1 NEPHI 17-20

19  1 NEPHI 21 - 2 NEPHI 2

20  2 NEPHI 3-6

21  2 NEPHI 7-10

22  2 NEPHI 11-14

23  ISAIAH TIPS (2 NEPHI 12&13)

24  ISAIAH TIPS (2 NEPHI 14&15)

25  2 NEPHI 15-18

26  ISAIAH TIPS (2 NEPHI 16-18)

27  ISAIAH TIPS (2 NEPHI 18cont.-20)

28  2 NEPHI 19-22

29  ISAIAH TIPS (2 NEPHI 21-25)

30  2 NEPHI 23-26

31  2 NEPHI 27-30

32  2 NEPHI 31 - JACOB 1

33  JACOB 2-5

34  JACOB 5 ILLUSTRATION

35  JACOB 5 ILLUSTRATION

36  JACOB 6 - JAROM 1

37  OMNI ILLUSTRATION

38  OMNI 1 - MOSIAH 2

39  MOSIAH 3-6

40  MOSIAH 7 ILLUSTRATION

41  MOSIAH 7-10

42  MOSIAH 11-14

43  ISAIAH TIPS (MOSIAH 14)

44  MOSIAH 15-18

# TABLE OF CONTENTS

45  MOSIAH 19-22

46  MOSIAH 23-26

47  MOSIAH 27-ALMA 1

48  ALMA 2-5

49  ALMA 6-9

50  ALMA 10-13

51  ALMA 14-17

52  ALMA 18-21

53  ALMA 22-25

54  ALMA 26-29

55  ALMA 30-33

56  ALMA 34-37

57  ALMA 38-41

58  ALMA 42-45

59  ALMA 46-49

60  ALMA 50-53

61  ALMA 54-57

62  ALMA 58-61

63  ALMA 62 - HELAMAN 2

64  HELAMAN 3-6

65  HELAMAN 7-10

66  HELAMAN 11-14

67  HELAMAN 15 - 3 NEPHI 2

68  3 NEPHI 3-6

69  3 NEPHI 7-10

70  3 NEPHI 11-14

71  3 NEPHI 15-18

72  3 NEPHI 19-22

73  3 NEPHI 23-26

74  3 NEPHI 27-30

75  4 NEPHI 1 - MORMON 3

76  MORMON 4-7

77  MORMON 8 - ETHER 2

78  ETHER 3-6

79  ETHER 7-10

80  ETHER 11-14

81  ETHER 15- MORONI 3

82  MORONI 4-7

83  MORONI 8-10

# BOOK OF MORMON READING CHART

**DATE STARTED:**

**FRONT OF THE BOOK OF MORMON**
- ○ TITLE PAGE  ○ TESTIMONY OF WITNESSES
- ○ TESTIMONY OF THE PROPHET JOSEPH SMITH
- ○ BRIEF EXPLANATION ABOUT THE BOOK OF MORMON

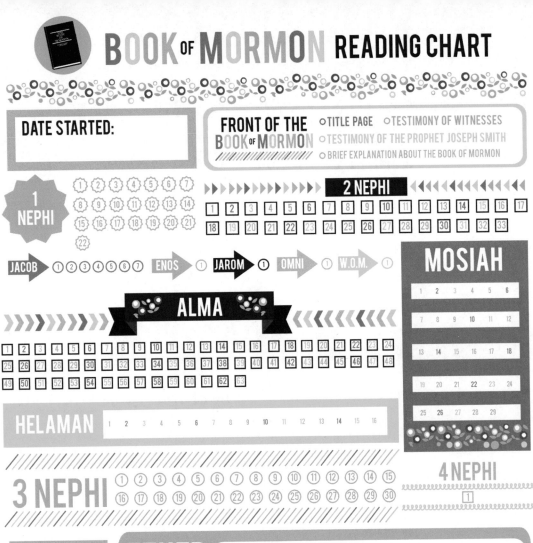

## 1 NEPHI
1 2 3 4 5 6 7 8 9 10 11 12 13 14 15 16 17 18 19 20 21 22

## 2 NEPHI
1 2 3 4 5 6 7 8 9 10 11 12 13 14 15 16 17 18 19 20 21 22 23 24 25 26 27 28 29 30 31 32 33

**JACOB** 1 2 3 4 5 6 7  **ENOS** 1  **JAROM** 1  **OMNI** 1  **W.O.M.** 1

## ALMA
1 2 3 4 5 6 7 8 9 10 11 12 13 14 15 16 17 18 19 20 21 22 23 24 25 26 27 28 29 30 31 32 33 34 35 36 37 38 39 40 41 42 43 44 45 46 47 48 49 50 51 52 53 54 55 56 57 58 59 60 61 62 63

## MOSIAH
1 2 3 4 5 6
7 8 9 10 11 12
13 14 15 16 17 18
19 20 21 22 23 24
25 26 27 28 29

## HELAMAN
1 2 3 4 5 6 7 8 9 10 11 12 13 14 15 16

## 3 NEPHI
1 2 3 4 5 6 7 8 9 10 11 12 13 14 15 16 17 18 19 20 21 22 23 24 25 26 27 28 29 30

## 4 NEPHI
1

## MORMON
1 2 3
4 5 6
7 8 9

## ETHER
1 2 3 4 5 6 7 8 9 10 11 12 13 14 15

## MORONI
1 2 3 4 5 6 7 8 9 10

**DATE FINISHED:**

# HOW TO USE THIS BOOK

AS YOU STUDY THE BOOK OF MORMON, USE THIS BOOK TO RECORD THINGS YOU LEARN IN EACH CHAPTER. PICK A FAVORITE DOCTRINE OR PRINCIPLE THAT STOOD OUT TO YOU AND RECORD IT, DOODLE A FAVORITE PHRASE, WRITE DOWN A LESSON YOU LEARNED. THERE IS NO RIGHT OR WRONG WAY!

RECORD A LESSON YOU LEARNED WHILE STUDYING THAT CHAPTER

ASK A THOUGHTFUL QUESTION

## 1 NEPHI 1

*lesson learned:*

The knowledge Lehi received gave him courage to testify in extremely difficult circumstances. Testimony is a source of strength and power!

*favorite scripture:* 1 Nephi 1:20

## 1 NEPHI 2

LESSON LEARNED:

What am i willing to sacrifice in order to obey the Lord's commandments?

Lehi left all of his material possessions and it began a story so great we are still learning from it !

FAVORITE SCRIPTURE: 1 Nephi 2:3-4

## 1 NEPHI 3

*lesson learned:*

I WILL GO and DO

Mission
Keep's commandments
temple
study scriptures
pray

THE THINGS WHICH THE LORD HATH COMMANDED

*favorite scripture:* 1 Nephi 3:7

## 1 NEPHI 4

LESSON LEARNED:

LET US BE strong LIKE UNTO MOSES

Moses was able to part the seas which was an immediate solution to a great problem in his day and with his people.
What can I do to be like him and, with the strength of the lord, change my circumstances rather than praying that the circmstances will change themselves?

FAVORITE SCRIPTURE: 1 Nephi 4:2

QUOTE A FAVORITE PHRASE

DRAW A FAVORITE PHRASE AND RECORD YOUR THOUGHTS

# BOOK OF MORMON
## PAGE TITLES

These titles are summaries of what is happening on each page in the Book of Mormon.
These titles can help in comprehension and make it easy to find things in your scriptures.
Just write the titles on the top of each page in your personal scriptures!

| Page | Title |
|---|---|
| 1 | Nephi's introduction, Jerusalem's dangerous political conditions |
| 2 | Lehi sees the future destruction of Jerusalem |
| 3 | Lehi warns the people |
| 4 | Lehi's family leaves Jerusalem |
| 5 | Lehi tells his sons to return to Jerusalem to get the brass plates from Laban |
| 6 | First attempt to get the plates |
| 7 | Second attempt to get the plates |
| 8 | Third attempt to get the plates |
| 9 | Zoram joins Nephi and his brothers |
| 10 | Lehi reads the plates |
| 11 | Nephi also keeps a record |
| 12 | Nephi and brothers return to Jerusalem to get wives |
| 13 | Laman and Lemuel rebel |
| 14 | Lehi's dream |
| 15 | Lehi's dream |
| 16 | Lehi's dream |
| 17 | Lehi prophesies |
| 18 | Nephi desires to see Lehi's dream himself |
| 19 | Nephi's vision (Nephi ponders and has a vision) |
| 20 | Nephi's vision (Tree of Life and Iron Rod) |
| 21 | Nephi's vision (The fall of the great and spacious building) |
| 22 | Nephi's vision (Mist of darkness) |
| 23 | Nephi's vision (River, mists, building, roads, gulf) |
| 24 | Nephi's vision (Christopher Columbus) |
| 25 | Nephi's vision (Coming forth of the Bible) |
| 26 | Nephi's vision (Coming forth of Book of Mormon) |
| 27 | Nephi's vision (Book of Mormon will establish truth of the Bible) |
| 28 | Nephi's vision (2 churches) |
| 29 | Nephi's vision (Saints persecuted by great and abominable church) |
| 30 | Nephi's vision (John the Beloved) |
| 31 | Nephi speaks to his brothers |
| 32 | Nephi explains Lehi's dream to his brothers |
| 33 | Nephi explains Lehi's dream to his brothers |
| 34 | Lehi receives the Liahona |
| 35 | The broken bow |
| 36 | Traveling eastward |
| 37 | Nephi is told to build a ship |
| 38 | Laman and Lemuel harden their hearts |
| 39 | Nephi teaches them from scripture |
| 40 | Nephi boldly testifies |
| 41 | The ship is finished |
| 42 | Cast off to sea |
| 43 | Laman and Lemuel tie up Nephi, arrival to Promised Land |
| 44 | Nephi makes 2 sets of plates |
| 45 | Prophecies of Christ |
| 46 | Nephi quotes Isaiah |
| 47 | Nephi quotes Isaiah |
| 48 | Nephi quotes Isaiah |
| 49 | Nephi quotes Isaiah, Nephi interprets Isaiah to his brothers |
| 50 | Nephi interprets Isaiah to his brothers |
| 51 | Gentiles will have the Gospel in the last days |
| 52 | Israel will be gathered |
| 53 | Nephi testifies |
| 54 | Lehi speaks to his rebellious sons: "Awake" |
| 55 | Lehi speaks to his rebellious sons: "Be men" |
| 56 | Lehi speaks to his rebellious sons: A Warning |
| 57 | Lehi speaks to Jacob: Redemption comes through Christ |
| 58 | Lehi speaks to Jacob: Opposition in all things |
| 59 | Lehi speaks to Jacob: We are free to choose |
| 60 | Lehi speaks to Joseph: Who he is named after |
| 61 | Lehi speaks to Joseph: Prophecy of Joseph Smith |
| 62 | Lehi blesses his posterity |
| 63 | Lehi dies, Nephi's psalm |
| 64 | Nephi's psalm |
| 65 | Nephites and Lamanites separate |
| 66 | Lamanites are cursed |
| 67 | Jacob and Joseph receive Priesthood authority, Jacob writes on the plates |
| 68 | Jacob quotes Isaiah: Israel will be scattered and then gathered |
| 69 | Jacob quotes Isaiah: A warning |
| 70 | Jacob quotes Isaiah: The Lord helps those who trust in Him |
| 71 | Jacob quotes Isaiah: In the last days Israel will be gathered |
| 72 | We need the resurrection |
| 73 | Why we need Christ |
| 74 | The Atonement saves us |
| 75 | The Atonement saves us |
| 76 | Remember Christ |
| 77 | Repent and prepare yourselves |
| 78 | The Jews will crucify Christ, be scattered and one day gathered |
| 79 | America will be a choice land |
| 80 | The Law of Moses points to Christ |
| 81 | Nephi quotes Isaiah: A latter-day temple |
| 82 | Nephi quotes Isaiah: Proud and lofty brought low at Second Coming |
| 83 | Nephi quotes Isaiah: Worldly daughters of Zion |
| 84 | Nephi quotes Isaiah: Scattering of Israel |
| 85 | Nephi quotes Isaiah: "But His hand is stretched out still" |
| 86 | Nephi quotes Isaiah: Isaiah sees the throne of God |
| 87 | Nephi quotes Isaiah: Prophecy and birth of Christ |
| 88 | Nephi quotes Isaiah: Seek the Lord |
| 89 | Nephi quotes Isaiah: Prophecy of the Messiah |
| 90 | Nephi quotes Isaiah: Destruction and the Second Coming |
| 91 | Nephi quotes Isaiah: The House of Israel shall return |
| 92 | Nephi quotes Isaiah: Christ will judge in righteousness |
| 93 | Nephi quotes Isaiah: The Millennial Day |
| 94 | The destruction of babylon |
| 95 | Nephi quotes Isaiah: Millennial rest |
| 96 | Nephi quotes Isaiah: Lucifer cast out |
| 97 | Nephi speaks of the importance of Isaiah |
| 98 | Jews will reject Christ and then be scattered |
| 99 | Jews will be restored when they believe in the Messiah |
| 100 | Why the Law of Moses was given |
| 101 | Chronological Prophecy |
| 102 | Last Days = Many Churches |
| 103 | Last Days = Priestcrafts vs. Charity |
| 104 | Nephi quotes Isaiah: Coming forth of the Book of Mormon |
| 105 | 3 Witnesses of the Book of Mormon |
| 106 | In the last days, the Lord will do a marvelous work |
| 107 | Satan's traps he uses |
| 108 | Satan's traps he uses |
| 109 | Warning to us |
| 110 | Last Days = Many will reject the Book of Mormon |
| 111 | Last Days: Many Jews and Gentiles will believe |
| 112 | The Millennium |
| 113 | The Doctrine of Christ |
| 114 | Faith, Repentance, Baptism, The Gift of the Holy Ghost, Endure to the End |
| 115 | The Holy Ghost |
| 116 | Nephi's words are true |
| 117 | Nephi's farewell |

1 NEPHI

2 NEPHI

| Page | Title |
|---|---|
| 118 | Come unto Christ and partake of his goodness |
| 119 | Jacob pleads with the Nephites to denounce wickedness |
| 120 | God before riches |
| 121 | The Lord delights in chastity |
| 122 | Jacob speaks to the righteous |
| 123 | Jacob's warnings |
| 124 | The Law of Moses points to Christ |
| 125 | Truth |
| 126 | Allegory of the olive tree |
| 127 | Allegory of the olive tree |
| 128 | Allegory of the olive tree |
| 129 | Allegory of the olive tree |
| 130 | Allegory of the olive tree |
| 131 | Allegory of the olive tree |
| 132 | Israel will be recovered in last days |
| 133 | Sherem denies Christ |
| 134 | Sherem desires a sign, then denies what he previously said |
| 135 | Nephite history. Jacob gives Enos the plates |
| 136 | Jacob's son, Enos' record |
| 137 | A lesson on prayer |
| 138 | Enos rejoices in Christ |
| 139 | Jarom's brief history |
| 140 | Passing the plates: Omni to Amaleki |
| 141 | King Mosiah discovers the people of Zarahemla |
| 142 | King Benjamin follows King Mosiah to the throne |
| 143 | Mormon's insert (notice date in corner) |
| 144 | Mormon kept a record for a "wise purpose" |
| 145 | King Benjamin teaches his sons |
| 146 | Mosiah chosen as next king of Zarahemla |
| 147 | King Benjamin calls his people to the temple |
| 148 | King Benjamin's sermon: Serve others |
| 149 | King Benjamin's sermon: Serve God |
| 150 | King Benjamin's sermon: A warning |
| 151 | King Benjamin's sermon: Keep the commandments |
| 152 | King Benjamin's sermon: The Atonement |
| 153 | King Benjamin's sermon: The natural man |
| 154 | King Benjamin's sermon: Judged according to our works |
| 155 | King Benjamin's sermon: Salvation comes through the Atonement |
| 156 | King Benjamin's sermon: Are we not all beggars? |
| 157 | King Benjamin's sermon: Watch yourselves |
| 158 | King Benjamin's sermon: Children of Christ |
| 159 | King Benjamin records names. He dies and Mosiah II is made king |
| 160 | Ammon and brethren brought before King Limhi |
| 161 | King Limhi speaks to his people |
| 162 | King Limhi speaks to his people |
| 163 | The 24 Jaredite plates |
| 164 | Zeniff's record |
| 165 | Zeniff's people move into the Land of Nephi |
| 166 | Zeniff's record: Peace and then battle – Nephites win |
| 167 | Zeniff's record: Why Lamanites hate Nephites |
| 168 | Wicked King Noah |
| 169 | Abinadi preaches - rejected by people |
| 170 | Abinadi prophesies |
| 171 | Abinadi taken before King Noah |
| 172 | Abinadi before King Noah and King Noah's wicked council |
| 173 | Abinadi's sermon to council |
| 174 | Abinadi's sermon |
| 175 | Abinadi's sermon |
| 176 | Abinadi's sermon |
| 177 | Abinadi's sermon |
| 178 | Abinadi's sermon |
| 179 | Alma believes Abinadi |
| 180 | Death of Abinadi |
| 181 | Alma escapes and preaches in private at the Waters of Mormon |
| 182 | Alma baptizes believers |
| 183 | Alma and people escape from King's army – Gideon tries to kill King Noah, Lamanites invade |
| 184 | King Noah's priests run away, King Noah killed |
| 185 | Limhi becomes king and establishes peace, King Noah's priests carry off Lamanite daughters |
| 186 | Limhi stops war with Lamanites |
| 187 | War again, Limhi's people turn to the Lord |
| 188 | Ammon and brethren find Limhi's people |
| 189 | Limhi and people desire to be baptized |
| 190 | Ammon helps Limhi's people escape and leads them to Zarahemla |
| 191 | Record of Alma's people who escaped from King Noah: Alma refuses to be their king |
| 192 | Alma and people become in bondage to Lamanites |
| 193 | Noah's wicked priest, Amulon, teaches the Lamanites and persecutes Alma |
| 194 | Alma and his people escape and go to Zarahemla |
| 195 | Mulekites become Nephites |
| 196 | Alma organizes church in Zarahemla |
| 197 | The Lord speaks to Alma |
| 198 | The Lord speaks to Alma |
| 199 | Alma the Younger and Sons of Mosiah persecute the church |
| 200 | Angel appears to Alma the Younger and Sons of Mosiah |
| 201 | Alma the Younger repents |
| 202 | Sons of Mosiah desire to preach the Gospel to the Lamanites |
| 203 | King Mosiah translates Jaredite plates |
| 204 | Judges instead of kings |
| 205 | King Mosiah's letter to his people |
| 206 | System of Judges |
| 207 | Alma and Mosiah die, Alma the Younger appointed as Chief Judge |
| 208 | Nehor introduces priestcraft and kills Gideon |
| 209 | Priestcraft and persecution spread |
| 210 | Believers vs. Nonbelievers |
| 211 | Amlici seeks to be king |
| 212 | Nephites conquer Amlicites and Amlicites join the Lamanites |
| 213 | Alma kills Amlici and Nephites drive back the Lamanites |
| 214 | Amlicites mark themselves |
| 215 | Nephites again drive back the Lamanites |
| 216 | Members of the church lifted up in pride |
| 217 | Nephihah appointed as Chief Judge. Alma still High Priest. |
| 218 | Alma's sermon: Questions we should ask ourselves |
| 219 | Alma's sermon: Questions that are meant to bring a change of heart |
| 220 | Alma's sermon: The Good Shepherd calls his people |
| 221 | Alma's sermon: Alma testifies |
| 222 | Alma's sermon: Will ye persist? |
| 223 | Success in Zarahemla |
| 224 | Alma's sermon in Gideon: The Spirit |
| 225 | Alma's sermon in Gideon: Prophecies of Christ |
| 226 | Alma's sermon in Gideon: What can and cannot enter the kingdom of God |
| 227 | Alma has success in Melek and then is rejected in Ammonihah, An angel appears to him |
| 228 | Alma meets Amulek |
| 229 | Alma preaches again in Ammonihah: Bold warnings |
| 230 | Alma's warnings to Ammonihah: What will happen if they continue to forsake the light |
| 231 | Alma's words to Ammonihah: The Lord is coming soon |
| 232 | Amulek's words to Ammonihah: He tells of the angel that appeared to him |
| 233 | Amulek's words to Ammonihah. Some try and trick Amulek, it doesn't work |
| 234 | Nephite coinage |
| 235 | Zeezrom tries to get Amulek to deny God by paying him money |
| 236 | Amulek vs. Zeezrom |
| 237 | Zeezrom silenced and caught in his lying. Alma uses opportunity to teach |
| 238 | Zeezrom asks sincere questions, Alma teaches about standing before God one day |
| 239 | Alma teaches about the Resurrection, Antionah asks questions |
| 240 | Alma teaches why we want to repent |
| 241 | Alma's words to Ammonihah: Priesthood holders foreordained in the premortal life |
| 242 | Alma's words to Ammonihah: Who Melchizedek was |
| 243 | Alma's words to Ammonihah: Christ is coming. Don't procrastinate your repentance |
| 244 | Alma and Amulek put into prison, believers in Ammonihah burned by fire |
| 245 | Alma and Amulek persecuted and mocked by judges, priests and others |
| 246 | Alma and Amulek break their cords, prison collapses, Alma and Amulek not hurt |

JACOB

ENOS

JAROM

OMNI

WORDS OF MORMON

MOSIAH

ALMA

ALMA

247   Alma and Amulek go to Sidom, Zeezrom is sick because of his iniquities, they heal him
248   Ammonihah destroyed by the Lamanites
249   Many go forth and preach the Gospel, churches established throughout land
250   Alma meets the sons of Mosiah in the wilderness, they tell their story
251   Sons of Mosiah go to preach the Gospel to the Lamanites Ammon goes to the land of Ishmael
252   Ammon becomes King Lamoni's servant
253   Ammon saves King's flocks
254   King Lamoni thinks Ammon is the Great Spirit
255   Ammon teaches King Lamoni who God is
256   King Lamoni believes and falls to the earth
257   Lamoni's household is converted. Abish teaches the people
258   Multitude argues about who Ammon is
259   Lamoni teaches his people, many baptized and become a righteous people
260   Ammon and King Lamoni go to rescue Ammon's imprisoned brothers, they meet Lamoni's father on the way
261   Alma delivers brethren from prison and the story of how they got there
262   Aaron teaches the Amalekites, he is rejected and put into prison
263   Aaron teaches Lamoni's father
264   Aaron teaches Lamoni's father, Lamoni's father desires to have eternal life
265   The King is converted and causes his people to be taught
266   Geography and how the land was divided
267   Lamanites in 7 lands are converted
268   Converted Lamanites change their name to Anti-Nephi-Lehies
269   As Lamanites prepare to come against the Anti-Nephi-Lehies, they bury their weapons
270   Anti-Nephi-Lehies slain without resistance, more Lamanites converted
271   Unconverted Lamanite's more angry with Nephites
272   More Lamanites converted
273   Ammon glories in the Lord
274   Ammon reflects on mission to the Lamanites
275   Ammon glories in the Lord
276   Anti-Nephi-Lehies leave Lamanite lands
277   Nephites give them the land of Jershon, Anti-Nephi-Lehies change their name to the People of Ammon
278   War
279   Alma's Psalm "O That I Were An Angel"
280   Continual peace
281   Korihor the Anti-Christ teaches there is no God, Christ, or Atonement
282   Nephite lands reject Korihor, he is taken before Alma
283   Alma questions Korihor and bears testimony to him
284   Korihor changes his position and eventually admits there is a God, he is struck dumb
285   Alma takes powerful missionaries to the Zoramites (apostate Nephites)
286   The Zoramites , their doctrine, and the Rameumptom
287   Alma's prayer about the Zoramites
288   Alma teaches the poor Zoramites
289   Alma teaches the poor Zoramites: Faith is not to have a perfect knowledge
290   Alma teaches the poor Zoramites: Faith is like a seed that can grow
291   Alma teaches the poor Zoramites: We can pray and worship God in all places
292   Alma teaches the poor Zoramites: Mercy comes through Christ
293   Amulek teaches the poor Zoramites: Why we need Christ
294   Alma teaches the poor Zoramites: The Law of Moses points to Christ
295   Alma teaches the poor Zoramites: Do not procrastinate your repentance
296   Popular Zoramites angry with Alma and other missionaries They cast those who listened to the missionaries out of the land
297   Angry Zoramites join with the Lamanites
298   Alma counsels his son Helaman: Tells of when he was young and wicked and the Angel appeared to him
299   Alma counsels his son Helaman: Alma's repentance process
300   Alma counsels his son Helaman: He gives the plates to Helaman
301   Alma counsels his son Helaman: Keep the commandments
302   Alma counsels his son Helaman: Talks about the record of the Jaredites
303   Alma counsels his son Helaman: Valuable advice
304   Alma counsels his son Shiblon: Alma's joy in his son
305   Alma counsels his son Shiblon: Bridle your passions
306   Alma counsels his son Corianton: Sexual sin is an abomination
307   Alma counsels his son Corianton: There will be a resurrection
308   Alma counsels his son Corianton: Where the spirits go to wait for the resurrection
309   Alma counsels his son Corianton: The resurrection, the wicked, the righteous
310   Alma counsels his son Corianton: Every person receives in the resurrection the same characteristics they acquired in mortality
311   Alma counsels his son Corianton: This is the time to repent
312   Alma counsels his son Corianton: The Fall and the Atonement
313   Alma counsels his son Corianton: Mercy is for those who repent
314   Zoramites become Lamanites
315   Lamanites come against the Nephites to war, Moroni arms the Nephites with armor
316   Battle
317   Nephites defend their homes, liberties, and families
318   Moroni commands the Lamanites to make a covenant of peace or die
319   Zerahemnah refuses, battle continues, Lamanites defeated
320   Alma prophecies the destruction of the Nephites
321   Alma the Younger is translated, problems grow in the Church
322   Amalickiah wants to be the king, he flatters many
323   Moroni raises the Title of Liberty, many follow and make covenant
324   Amalickiah and his followers flee to Lamanite land
325   Moroni plants Title of Liberty as a standard, peace in the land
326   Amalickiah conspires to become the king of the Lamanites
327   Amalickiah begins by cunningly becoming a leader in his army, he has his servants kill the king
328   Amalickiah marries the queen and becomes king of the Lamanites, he Inspires them to go to war against the Nephites
329   Moroni prepares his people, if all men would be like Moroni, Satan would have no power
330   Nephites attitude towards war, Nephite preparations
331   Amalickiah's attitude towards war, Lamanites can't attack, Nephites too prepared
332   Nephites had power over enemies, Amalickiah filled with hatred – swears to drink Moroni's blood
333   Moroni continues to fortify his cities
334   Many new Nephite cities built, peaceful years, a group of Nephites battle with other Nephites
335   Teancum vs Morianton, people of Morianton covenant to keep peace
336   Pahoran becomes Chief Judge of Nephites, some Nephites want a king instead of judges, They are called "King Men", others are "Free Men"
337   Amalickiah comes again against the Nephites, King Men refuse to defend their country, King Men compelled to fight
338   Lamanites take many Nephite cities
339   Teancum slays Amalickiah, Amalickiah's brother, Ammoron, becomes king
340   Preparations for war
341   Nephites take back one of their cities
342   City of Mulek made stronger
343   Helaman becomes leader of 2000 stripling warriors
344   Moroni's letter to Ammoron
345   Ammoron's letter to Moroni
346   Moroni refuses to exchange prisoners, his plan to free the Nephite prisoners
347   Prisoners freed, another Nephite city taken back
348   Helaman's letter to Moroni telling him about the war he is fighting
349   Antipus and Helaman fight together with their armies
350   The faith of the 2000 stripling warriors
351   Not one of the 2000 die in battle
352   The battle continues
353   All of the 2000 are wounded, but none are killed
354   More battle
355   More battle
356   More battle, Helaman takes back another Nephite city
357   Moroni asks Pahoran to send men to strengthen Helaman, more battle
358   Moroni sends a letter to Pahoran rebuking him for not sending men

| Page | Title |
|------|-------|

**ALMA**

| Page | Title |
|------|-------|
| 359 | Moroni's letter to Pahoran |
| 360 | Moroni's letter to Pahoran, he threatens to fight against the government |
| 361 | Pahoran's response, he explains that he has been facing rebellion against the government |
| 362 | The King Men have taken over Zarahemla and appointed a king |
| 363 | Moroni marches to aid Pahoran, thousands join him, Pahoran is restored to his judgment seat |
| 364 | Another Nephite city retaken from Lamanites, Lamanite prisoners covenant to not war any longer, they join the people of Ammon |
| 365 | Ammoron killed |
| 366 | Lamanites driven from land. Peace established. Helaman dies. |
| 367 | Hagoth leads many Nephites by boat to a land northward, Moroni dies, Shiblon dies, records passed to Helaman's son Helaman |

**HELAMAN**

| Page | Title |
|------|-------|
| 368 | Pahoran appointed Chief Judge |
| 369 | Chief Judge murdered, Secret combinations form |
| 370 | War |
| 371 | Gadianton |
| 372 | Nephites prosper and migrate northward |
| 373 | Account of records, Helaman becomes Chief Judge |
| 374 | Church grows, Nephi becomes Chief Judge, pride enters church |
| 375 | Wicked Nephites and Lamanites conquer land of Zarahemla |
| 376 | "The judgments of God did stare them in the face," Nephites conquered because of wickedness |
| 377 | Nephi passes judgment seat to Cezoram, Nephi and Lehi go out and preach |
| 378 | "Remember," many repent and are baptized |
| 379 | Nephi and Lehi put into prison- they are encircled by fire, a Voice speaks |
| 380 | Lamanites preach to Nephites, they prosper |
| 381 | Cezoram is murdered. Pride enters, Gadianton Robbers |
| 382 | Gadianton Robbers |
| 383 | Lucifer is author of wickedness |
| 384 | Lamanites destroy Gadianton Robbers among them, Nephites build them up, Nephi preaches and is rejected |
| 385 | Nephi's prayer on the garden tower |
| 386 | Corrupt judges try and turn the people against Nephi |
| 387 | All the prophets taught what Nephi is teaching – so why are they rejecting Nephi? |
| 388 | By inspiration, Nephi announces the murder of the Chief Judge |
| 389 | Chief Judge found murdered |
| 390 | Nephi tells who murdered the Chief Judge |
| 391 | Nephi accepted by some as a prophet |
| 392 | Nephi given the sealing power |
| 393 | Many die from famine, they are humbled and repent |
| 394 | Famine ends, there is peace |
| 395 | Gadianton robbers become exceedingly great, they cause great havoc |
| 396 | How foolish man can be… |
| 397 | Samuel the Lamanite preaches and is cast out |
| 398 | Samuel the Lamanites words as he stands upon the city's wall |
| 399 | Samuel the Lamanite: What kind of a prophet do you want? |
| 400 | Samuel the Lamanite: You will soon realize this |
| 401 | Samuel the Lamanite: Signs of Christ's birth |
| 402 | Samuel the Lamanite: Signs of Christ's death |
| 403 | Samuel the Lamanite: Nephites are being chastened |
| 404 | Samuel the Lamanite: Warnings |
| 405 | Many baptized, some try to kill Samuel but he could not be slain |

**3 NEPHI**

| Page | Title |
|------|-------|
| 406 | Some say it is not reasonable to believe in Christ |
| 407 | Even though there are many signs, unbelievers set apart a day to put to death those who believe |
| 408 | Sign of Christ's birth comes, many believe, others lie and deceive |
| 409 | Gadianton robbers' children join them, people begin to forget the signs |
| 410 | Lamanites and Nephites unite to defend themselves against the Gadianton robbers |
| 411 | Giddianhi's (Gadianton leader) letter to Lachoneus (Nephite Governor or Chief Judge) demanding them to surrender |
| 412 | Lachoneus could not be threatened, he prepares his people, appoints Gidgiddoni as chief captain (like Moroni) |
| 413 | Nephite armies defeat Gadianton Robbers |
| 414 | Gadianton leader, Giddianhi, is slain |
| 415 | Giddianhi's successor, Zemnarihah was hanged |

**3 NEPHI**

| Page | Title |
|------|-------|
| 416 | Nephites repent |
| 417 | Mormon's words |
| 418 | Nephite's prosper, pride, class distinctions, inequality |
| 419 | Prophets preach repentance and are killed in secret, secret combinations arise |
| 420 | Government is overthrown, everyone divides into tribes |
| 421 | Nephi preaches, and there are many great miracles |
| 422 | Signs of Christ's death |
| 423 | Signs of Christ's death, people wish they had repented |
| 424 | Christ's voice is heard in the darkness |
| 425 | He proclaims who he is |
| 426 | Christ promises to gather his people |
| 427 | More righteous part of people have been preserved |
| 428 | Christ appears to the Nephites |
| 429 | One by one they feel the marks of the Atonement, Christ teaches the manner of baptism |
| 430 | Christ's doctrine |
| 431 | Christ calls the Twelve, He gives a sermon similar to one the gave to the Jews in Matt 5 |
| 432 | The Higher Law |
| 433 | The Higher Law, be perfect |
| 434 | How to pray, forgiveness, fasting, real treasures, serving God |
| 435 | Trust God, seek His kingdom first, judge not, ask, seek, knock; Golden Rule |
| 436 | Strait and narrow, beware of false prophets, wise man vs. foolish man |
| 437 | Law of Moses is fulfilled, Christ is the law, He speaks to the disciples |
| 438 | They are his "other sheep" and he still has others that he will go to and he will gather them |
| 439 | In the last days the truth will go forth |
| 440 | Christ tells them to go home and ponder his words, they don't want him to leave, He heals their sick |
| 441 | Little children brought to him, entire multitude kneels and Christ prays, His joy is full, He weeps, angels encircle the children |
| 442 | Sacrament instituted |
| 443 | Pray unto the Father in His name, don't take sacrament unworthily |
| 444 | Disciples given power to confer Holy Ghost, Christ ascends to Heaven, everyone goes to their homes and announces what has happened |
| 445 | Disciples named, they teach the people exactly what they had been taught, disciples baptized, angels come, Jesus comes |
| 446 | Jesus prays, the disciples pray, Jesus prays again |
| 447 | Jesus administers the sacrament again, Israel will be gathered |
| 448 | The Americas will be established and will be a New Jerusalem, Israel will inherit it and bless the nations |
| 449 | The fullness of My Gospel will be preached to Israel and they will believe |
| 450 | Israel will be gathered when the Book of Mormon comes forth, Gentiles will be a free people in America |
| 451 | Promises and warnings to those Gentiles |
| 452 | Israel will build a New Jerusalem, lost tribes will return |
| 453 | Zion will be established |
| 454 | We should study Isaiah, He looks at Nephite records and has them add Samuel's words to them |
| 455 | Christ quotes Malachi, tithing |
| 456 | Proud will be burned at Second Coming, Elijah will return before then |
| 457 | Christ truly taught the people and then ascended to the Father |
| 458 | They were called the Church of Christ and everything they do should be in His name |
| 459 | "This is my gospel…" |
| 460 | Do these things |
| 461 | The 3 Nephites |
| 462 | 3 Translated Nephites |
| 463 | The Book of Mormon coming forth is a sign that the Lord is gathering Israel |

**MORMON / 4 NEPHI**

| Page | Title |
|------|-------|
| 464 | Mormon speaks to us in the last days |
| 465 | What a Zion society is like |
| 466 | What a Zion society is like (for almost 200 years) |
| 467 | Wickedness and division among the people |
| 468 | Nephites, Lamanites, and Gadianton… AGAIN! |
| 469 | Ammaron instructs Mormon about plates…. war |
| 470 | Wickedness among Nephites, Mormon leads Nephite armies |
| 471 | Mormon obtains plates |

| Page | Title |
|------|-------|

**MORMON**

| | |
|------|-------|
| 472 | War |
| 473 | Mormon cries repentance |
| 474 | War |
| 475 | Indescribable war |
| 476 | War |
| 477 | The Book of Mormon will come forth in due time |
| 478 | The Land of Cumorah |
| 479 | The Last Battle |
| 480 | Mormon's final words |
| 481 | Moroni remains alone |
| 482 | The Book of Mormon |
| 483 | Moroni speaks to our day |
| 484 | Moroni speaks to those who do not believe in Christ |
| 485 | Moroni shows who God is |
| 486 | Be wise in this life |
| 487 | Moroni speaks of this record |

**ETHER**

| | |
|------|-------|
| 488 | Tower of Babel |
| 489 | Brother of Jared is directed by the Lord |
| 490 | Jaredites promised a land |
| 491 | The barges, no air, no light |
| 492 | The brother of Jared sees the finger of the Lord |
| 493 | The brother of Jared sees the Lord |
| 494 | The brother of Jared's vision |
| 495 | Have faith as the brother of Jared |
| 496 | 3 Witnesses of the Book of Mormon |
| 497 | Jaredites on the water for 344 days |
| 498 | Oriah made king. Jared and his brother die |
| 499 | Strife amongst the Jaredites |
| 500 | Contention over the kingdom |
| 501 | Secret combinations |
| 502 | Kingdom passes by descent or murder |
| 503 | Righteous King – peace and prosperity in land |
| 504 | Wickedness in land...plagues |
| 505 | Succession of Kings, some righteous, some wicked |
| 506 | Righteousness = blessings |
| 507 | Wickedness and war, prophets warn of destruction |
| 508 | Prophets rejected by the people |
| 509 | Ether is prophet, teaches of Faith |
| 510 | FAITH |
| 511 | Faith, Hope, and Charity |
| 512 | The New Jerusalem to be built in America |
| 513 | Ether prophecies of a great war amongst the Jaredites |
| 514 | The land is cursed |
| 515 | Great war |
| 516 | The final battle – millions die |
| 517 | "Men, women, and children being armed with weapons of war" |
| 518 | Jaredites utterly destroyed |

**MORONI**

| | |
|------|-------|
| 519 | Priesthood ordination and ordinances |
| 520 | Baptism, repentance, forgiveness, church meetings |
| 521 | Moroni speaks to members of the church |
| 522 | Judging |
| 523 | Faith |
| 524 | Charity |
| 525 | Mormon's letter to Moroni: When children should be baptized |
| 526 | Mormon's letter to Moroni: Little children |
| 527 | Mormon's 2nd Letter to Moroni: What the Nephites and Lamanites were like |
| 528 | Mormon's 2nd Letter to Moroni: The horrible scene |
| 529 | Moroni's promise – how to know the Book of Mormon is true |
| 530 | The gifts of the spirit |
| 531 | Come unto Christ |

# 1 NEPHI 1

LESSON LEARNED:

FAVORITE SCRIPTURE:

# 1 NEPHI 2

LESSON LEARNED:

FAVORITE SCRIPTURE:

# 1 NEPHI 3

LESSON LEARNED:

FAVORITE SCRIPTURE:

# 1 NEPHI 4

LESSON LEARNED:

FAVORITE SCRIPTURE:

# 1 NEPHI 5

**LESSON LEARNED:**

**FAVORITE SCRIPTURE:**

## 1 NEPHI 6

**LESSON LEARNED:**

**FAVORITE SCRIPTURE:**

# 1 NEPHI 7

**LESSON LEARNED:**

**FAVORITE SCRIPTURE:**

# 1 NEPHI 8

**LESSON LEARNED:**

**FAVORITE SCRIPTURE:**

# WHAT IS "THE HOUSE OF ISRAEL"?

## ABRAHAM

Abraham was a great prophet who made a covenant with God called "The Abrahamic Covenant"

## THE ABRAHAMIC COVENANT

This was a very important covenant. The Abrahamic Covenant includes all Gospel covenants, and thus promised Abraham the ability to gain eternal life. In return, Abraham promised to bear the Priesthood and teach the Gospel to the rest of God's children

## Abraham's Family

Abraham was promised that this covenant would be renewed with all of his posterity. So they would all have the covenants of eternal life and the responsibility to teach the rest of God's children.

### This is Abraham's Family

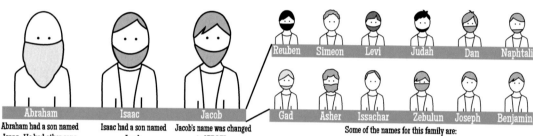

Reuben   Simeon   Levi   Judah   Dan   Naphtali

Gad   Asher   Issachar   Zebulun   Joseph   Benjamin

**Abraham**
Abraham had a son named Isaac. He had other sons too, but Isaac was the "birthright" son and was the next prophet.

**Isaac**
Isaac had a son named Jacob.

**Jacob**
Jacob's name was changed to ISRAEL. Israel had 12 sons.

Some of the names for this family are:
THE HOUSE OF ISRAEL
THE CHILDREN OF ISRAEL
ISRAELITES

---

The below explanations can help you understand the House of Israel and what has happened to them (us) over the years. As you study, doodle your thoughts and questions all over the page and map.

We are of the Tribe of Judah

I am of the Tribe of Asher

I am of the Tribe of Simeon

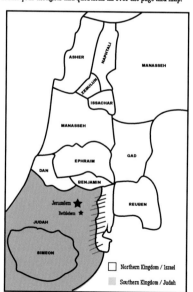

Jerusalem ★
Bethlehem ★

JUDAH

SIMEON

☐ Northern Kingdom / Israel
▨ Southern Kingdom / Judah

For generations after, all Israelites knew from which of the 12 sons they descended from. Each son had his own "tribe" made up of his descendants. So one may have been of the "Tribe of Judah" and another the "Tribe of Asher". Out of the 12 sons, Joseph was the "birthright" son, and so he stood at the head of his family. He had two sons: Ephraim and Manasseh. Joseph's descendants specifically identified themselves through his sons. So his descendants would be of the "Tribe of Ephraim" or the "Tribe of Manasseh". The Land of Israel was divided and each tribe inherited a portion of the land. Jerusalem was the capital city and where the temple was.

Over time, the Israelites decided they wanted a king like the other nations had. The Prophet Samuel warned them against having a king because wicked kings would corrupt the people God had chosen to be examples to the rest of His children. However, the people decided they wanted a king any way.

The Israelites had many kings over many generations. Some kings were righteous, and others were very wicked. Eventually, there arose a divide among the people and 10 tribes split from 2 of the tribes (Judah and Benjamin).

The 10 tribes will be known as the Northern Tribes or the "Kingdom of Israel" and they will have their own king. The other 2 tribes will be known as the "Southern Tribes" or the "Kingdom of Judah" (or the Jews) and their own king. The Kingdom of Judah will have the capital city of Jerusalem.

Over time the Northern tribe became increasingly wicked until they no longer had God's protection. The Assyrians eventually capture them and carry many of them off to other nations. There, they will eventually become like those nations and worship as those nations worship. From thenceforth, they will be known as the "lost tribes of Israel" and are likened unto sheep who are lost and scattered from their flock. The Prophets will then write of a day when their people will be "gathered" back as descendants of Abraham and the covenant they are heirs to. In fact, the majority of the last part of the Bible is all about this, as well as the Book of Mormon.

This gathering has begun in these last days. Individuals are gathered one at a time as they are baptized. They will then, at some point, receive their Patriarchal Blessing which will declare which of the 12 tribes they have descended from.

At the beginning of the Book of Mormon, Lehi is living in Jerusalem and the Northern tribe has already been captured by Assyria; and now the Southern tribes are risking captivity by the Babylonians.

After Lehi departs, Babylon does capture the Kingdom of Judah and carries many off to Babylon (like Daniel, Shedrach, Meshach, and Abed-Nego). However, eventually Judah later returned to Israel and rebuilt their land. Christ was born after these events and during a time the Romans had power over Israel.

# LIKE AN OLIVE TREE...

Wild Tree

Branch of Healthy Tree

The House of Israel is often compared to an olive tree.

"Grafting" was a common practice in ancient times where you would take a branch from one tree and insert it into a different tree.

One purpose of doing this might be to help an olive tree which was no longer bearing fruit. One would take a branch from a healthy tree and "Graft" it into the wild tree in hopes that it would strengthen the tree.

Sometimes the House of Israel is compared to the branches that are grafted into the wild tree. Other times the House of Israel is compared to the wild tree that once bore fruit and the Lord is trying to strengthen again. And other times, the House of Israel is like a scattered or lost branch being inserted into the true tree.

# WHAT IS A "GENTILE"?

The Book of Mormon often refers to "Gentiles," but what is a Gentile?

| |
|---|
| Look up "Gentile" in your Bible Dictionary. Write the first sentence of the defintion here: |

| |
|---|
| What are the two common uses of the word Gentile (first paragraph in your Bible Dicionary under "Gentile")? |

Example:

Lehi

King Nebuchadnezzar's Army

Israelite      Gentile

Circle which one of the two uses is commonly used in the Book of Mormon (explained in the last sentence of the first paragraph in your Bible Dictionary).

# 1 NEPHI 9

LESSON LEARNED:

FAVORITE SCRIPTURE:

# 1 NEPHI 10

LESSON LEARNED:

*Study pages 14 and 15 before you fill in this square.

FAVORITE SCRIPTURE:

# 1 NEPHI 11

LESSON LEARNED:

FAVORITE SCRIPTURE:

# 1 NEPHI 12

LESSON LEARNED:

FAVORITE SCRIPTURE:

# 1 NEPHI 13

LESSON LEARNED:

FAVORITE SCRIPTURE:

# 1 NEPHI 14

LESSON LEARNED:

FAVORITE SCRIPTURE:

# 1 NEPHI 15

LESSON LEARNED:

FAVORITE SCRIPTURE:

# 1 NEPHI 16

LESSON LEARNED:

FAVORITE SCRIPTURE:

# 1 NEPHI 17

LESSON LEARNED:

FAVORITE SCRIPTURE:

**1 NEPHI 19**

LESSON LEARNED:

FAVORITE SCRIPTURE:

# 1 NEPHI 18

LESSON LEARNED:

FAVORITE SCRIPTURE:

**1 NEPHI 20**

LESSON LEARNED:

FAVORITE SCRIPTURE:

# 1 NEPHI 21

LESSON LEARNED:

FAVORITE SCRIPTURE:

# 1 NEPHI 22

LESSON LEARNED:

FAVORITE SCRIPTURE:

# ♥ 2 NEPHI 1 ♥

LESSON LEARNED:

FAVORITE SCRIPTURE:

# 2 NEPHI 2

LESSON LEARNED:

FAVORITE SCRIPTURE:

## 2 NEPHI 3

FAVORITE SCRIPTURE

## 2 NEPHI 4

LESSON LEARNED:

FAVORITE SCRIPTURE:

## 2 NEPHI 5

LESSON LEARNED:

FAVORITE SCRIPTURE:

## 2 NEPHI 6

LESSON LEARNED:

FAVORITE SCRIPTURE:

# 2 NEPHI 7

LESSON LEARNED

FAVORITE SCRIPTURE

# 2 NEPHI 8

LESSON LEARNED:

FAVORITE SCRIPTURE:

# 2 NEPHI 9

LESSON LEARNED:

FAVORITE SCRIPTURE:

# 2 NEPHI 10

LESSON LEARNED:

FAVORITE SCRIPTURE:

## 2 NEPHI 11

LESSON LEARNED:

♥♥♥♥♥♥♥♥♥♥♥♥♥♥♥♥♥♥♥♥♥♥♥♥♥♥♥♥♥♥♥♥♥

FAVORITE SCRIPTURE:

* 2 Nephi chapters 12-24 are know as "Isaiah chapters" because Nephi is quoting Isaiah. Nephi had Isaiah's words on the Brass Plates, we have Isaiah's words in the Old Testament. Isaiah wrote with a lot of imagery and symbolism. When understood, the symbolism can teach you with greater power and clarity than if symbolism was not used. Turn to page 23 to find tips for understanding this chapter (2 Nephi 12). Tips for all of the Isaiah chapters are provided. You can use these tips as you study 2 Nephi 12-24.

 ## 2 NEPHI 12

LESSON LEARNED:

FAVORITE SCRIPTURE:

## 2 NEPHI 13

LESSON LEARNED:

FAVORITE SCRIPTURE:

## 2 NEPHI 14

LESSON LEARNED:

FAVORITE SCRIPTURE:

# 2 NEPHI TIPS

## 2 NEPHI 12

> **TIP** ▶ For the next several chapters, Nephi quotes Isaiah. We have Isaiah in our Old Testament. Nephi had his words on the Brass Plates.

Verse 1 — In Hebrew, "word" can also be translated as "message".

Verse 2 — - A mountain is symbolic of a high place where God comes to communicate with His people.
- The term "when" suggests that the temple needed to be built in order for the events to follow.

Verse 3 — These are events that will occur and/or precede the Millennium. Temples will cover the earth, but two great temples will be built. One in the New Jerusalem ("Zion") and the other in Old Jerusalem ("Jerusalem").

Verse 4 — Notice that the rebuking in this verse causes positive change.

Verses 5-6 — - House of Jacob = House of Israel
- One Hebrew translation for "forsaken" means to disperse or spread about.
- "Replenished from the east": Anciently, east was a sacred direction. These verses suggest they are looking to other sources for spiritual guidance.
- Another translation for "please themselves" is "clasp hands".

Verses 7-9 — These verses describe the state of the people and their society.

Verses 10-12 — These verses explain what the consequences will be for the people.

Verse 13 — "Cedars of Lebanon" and "Oaks of Bashan" were both trees that produced highly valued wood used for fancy furniture and buildings.

Verse 16 — The ships that Isaiah is referencing were commercial ships. The Ships of Tarshish were likely from a region in Spain, and these ships were known for being especially strong and able to withstand the forces of the sea. Pleasant pictures were the statues or standards at the heads of the ships.

Verse 19 — "To shake terribly the earth": This could literally mean that there will be a great earthquake, or it could mean that all of the values and prideful things of the world will come falling down.

Verses 20-21 — "To the moles and to the bats": These are animals that cannot see and certainly would not value these items.

Verse 22 — This verse emphasizes the frailty of man, of which the people are placing all of their trust. They are putting all of their faith in the hands of man, when he is always a breath away from death.

## 2 NEPHI 13

> **TIP** ▶ In this chapter, Nephi continues to quote Isaiah. Isaiah is teaching about the consequences which will come upon the wicked.

Verse 1 — "Stay and staff" means that the whole supply of bread and water will be taken away.

Verses 2-3 — These verses are referring to men and women who aspire to high positions.

Verse 4 — Rather than experienced leaders, young and inexperienced men will be placed in these leadership positions.
The 7 kings following Isaiah's death (Manasseh, Amon, Josiah, Jehoahaz, Jehoiakim, Jehoiachin, and Zedekiah) all became kings between the ages of 8-25.

Verse 5 — In such a state of wickedness and poor leadership, chaos ensues and there is a disrespect towards the older generations. There is also a state of oppression and competition among neighbors.

Verses 6-7 — Brothers are looking for leadership in the family because the father has either died in war or abandoned his family.
They are not mentioning that they are taking hold of the older brother to rule the family but rather someone who at least has clothing. Each brother is refusing the role to lead.

Verses 8-9 — The reasons that Jerusalem will be destroyed. People cannot hide their sins. It shows in their countenance.

Verse 12 — This verse refers to the organization and partnership of the family. Some scholars have also suggested that "women" in this context could be used to describe cowardly men.

Verses 13-15 — The Lord is chastising the people for a lack of compassion and charity given to those in need; and in fact, make life more difficult for those who are suffering.

Verses 16-17 — - Scholars agree that "daughter of Zion" refers to one who lived in Jerusalem during Isaiah's day. Daughters of Zion (plural) could refer to his day as well as the last days.
- Isaiah is describing the covenant daughters of Zion, who rather than keeping themselves pure and modest, are adorning themselves to look as the women of the world or their neighboring countries.
- Many of the fashions of Isaiah's day are different than today; however, women (and men) choosing fashions to appear a certain way is a timeless issue.
- In these (and the following verses) Isaiah specifically mentions ladies' jewelry and fashions that were popular in his day. Although it may be intriguing to discuss what each thing may have been, or what it could have looked like, the important principle is that the things she places so much value, time, and energy on has no eternal significance and will not sustain her.
- "Smite with a scab the crown of the head" means to cause a disease of the scalp which would result in baldness. Hence, their appearance, which they value so much, will be taken away, or will not offer her happiness.

Verses 18-23 — In Isaiah's day, the poor wore clothing made from their own sheep and often went without shoes. Isaiah is exposing the upper class of women who flaunt their jewelry and ornaments and take on the fashions of neighboring countries.

Verse 24 — The details of this verse paints a picture of someone who is in mourning. In Isaiah's day, if someone was in mourning they would rent (rip) their clothing, shave their head, put on clothing made of sack cloth (an itchy material), and sit on the ground and sprinkle ashes over their head. They were outwardly doing things that expressed how they felt inwardly.

Verses 25-26 — "Sit upon the ground" suggests that these women will be in great mourning. Where do we go when in distress? Often to the ground or lowest point.

# 2 NEPHI 14

TIP In this chapter, Nephi continues to quote Isaiah. Isaiah is teaching about Zion and the Millennium.

Verse 1
- Many scholars suggest that this verse could have been placed at the end of the previous chapter.
- In Isaiah's day, it was disgraceful to be unmarried and childless. Due to the loss of men (through war or other means), the women ask the men to marry them without needing to fulfill the man's responsibility of providing for their needs.

Verse 2
- Chapter 13 teaches about the widespread wickedness, pride, and despair. Chapter 14 prophesies of the redemption and cleansing of Israel and the establishment of Zion, even in the midst of a wicked world. There is a stark contrast between the despair of the world and hope in Christ and Zion.
- The branch can either represent Christ or the House of Israel.

Verse 3
There are those who have abandoned the ways of the world and have had it's filth washed away.

Verse 5
"Upon every dwelling place": this can represent every church, temple, and home.
"Cloud and smoke": this is a protection for those in Zion from the heat or consequences of the world. This cloud would also shield the world from the glory of the Lord that is within the dwelling places.

Verse 6
Zion will be a place of refuge or the only place of peace and protection during a time that the world is in great turmoil.

# 2 NEPHI 15

TIP In this chapter, Nephi continues to quote Isaiah. At the beginning of this chapter Isaiah is comparing the House of Israel to a vineyard.

Verse 1
- This chapter uses the vineyard and the grapevines in the vineyard to represent the House of Israel.
- The grapevine is capable of producing a lot of fruit if given the required care and attention. If left uncared for, it will seldom survive.
- These characteristics made the grapevine a good comparison to the House of Israel.
- The "well-beloved" is Christ who his caring for this vineyard (the House of Israel).

Verse 2
It was a very fruitful hill where the vineyard was planted. The result should have been an abundant harvest, but instead wild grapes grew.

Verse 5
Since this vineyard failed to produce, this is what will happen to it.

TIP Verses 8-23 proclaim six woeful behaviors and consequences among the House of Israel.

Verses 8-9
**Wo #1**
Wealthy land owners would buy up all of the property they could until their borders met up with one another's. This violated the Law of Jubilee which protected people from being enslaved to the wealthy who had no intention of using the land for good. * See Bible Dictionary: "Jubilee, Year of"

Verse 10
The consequence is that these lands would become extremely unproductive.
1 Homer = 10 Ephah.    Therefore, the land owner would get 1/10th back of what he planted; and, therefore, would have a great loss.
1 Bath = 4-8 gallons of wine.    4-8 gallons of wine over 10 acres of land is a ridiculously small harvest.

Verses 11-12
**Wo #2**
Isaiah is describing people who were the "partiers" of his day. The musical instruments were used in worship, but these people were using them at their feasts.

Verses 13-14
The result is a spiritual and intellectual famine among the people. Hell, who has deceived them all along, will happily receive them.

Verse 17
Isaiah has taught about the waste of land and the waste of intellect. These places and people are left desolate. Imagine a desolate field which has stopped producing fruit or crop. What is left? Forage for lambs and young goats ("strangers" can be translated as young goats).

Verses 18-19
**Wo #3**
- A cart rope is a rope that is pulling a cart filled with something. Here, the rope is pulling sin and vanity.
- "That we may see it" means that they are sign seekers. They are telling the Lord to hurry and show them so that they can know it.

Verse 20
**Wo #4**
The great switch of values and change of perception of good and evil.

Verse 21
**Wo #5**

Verses 22-23
**Wo #6**
"Who justify the wicked for reward" are those who take bribes. Verse 22 teaches about alcohol or harmful products. Some scholars suggest that Isaiah is referring to those in our day who will promote dangerous or immoral products in exchange for large amounts of money. This type of advertising, especially when targeting youth, leads individuals away from righteousness.

Verses 24-26
- When a farmer has gathered his grain, he would wait for a windy day and "winnow" his grain. He did this to separate the seeds from the "chaff" and "stubble". He would gather it and toss it in the air. The wind would then blow the lighter chaff and stubble away while the seed would fall back to the ground. Once the farmer gathered his seed, he would burn the chaff and stubble with a fire that would grow extremely fast. Isaiah is likening the fate of the chaff and stubble to those who fall within the 6 woes.
- An ensign is a flag or "standard" raised during times of battle.
- The Hebrew translation for "hiss" is to quietly proclaim.

Verses 27-30
- Isaiah is describing the speed and haste in which the people will gather. Many scholars suggest that Isaiah is trying to describe the transportation of the last days and how the people can arrive in little time, without stopping to sleep.
- The quality of a horse depended, partly, on how hard their hooves were. Flint is a hard type of quartz.
- Many scholars suggest that Isaiah was seeing an unstoppable, powerful means of transportation. The wheels of a whirlwind could be a train and the roaring of a lion could be a plane's powerful engine.

# 2 NEPHI 15

LESSON LEARNED:

FAVORITE SCRIPTURE:

# 2 NEPHI 16

LESSON LEARNED:

FAVORITE SCRIPTURE:

## 2 NEPHI 17

LESSON LEARNED:

FAVORITE SCRIPTURE:

# 2 NEPHI 18

LESSON LEARNED:

FAVORITE SCRIPTURE:

# 2 NEPHI 16

TIP In this chapter, Nephi continues to quote Isaiah. Isaiah is writing about his calling to become the prophet.

**Verse 1**
-Isaiah is having a vision and will attempt to describe what he is seeing using figurative language. This is often how prophets seek to explain the grandeur and splendor of such a moment.
- Consider each thing literally and figuratively. For example, was the Lord actually sitting upon a throne? Maybe, maybe not. If not, what would the throne represent?
- A train is something that follows behind, like a train on a wedding gown. The longer the train, the greater the symbol of glory. The train could also represent the Lord's followers.

**Verse 2**
Wings are symbols of power, and these beings had three sets of these wings. One set covered their faces, another set covered their feet, and with the last set they could fly.

**Verses 3-4**
- These seraphim cried with such power that the posts of the door shook. The doorway should be the most solid part of the building, and even this is moved by the power of these voices. The smoke could represent the prayers sent up from earth. In the ancient tabernacles, the Priests would stand before the Altar of Incense and pray in behalf of the Children of Israel. That smoke arising up from the altar was representative of their prayers going up to heaven. Here, Isaiah sees that the prayers have made it before the Lord.

**Verses 5-7**
Isaiah looks around and realizes that he feels out of place there. He is un-done, or not ready. The live, or hot, coal from the altar would have come from the Altar of Sacrifice which was representative of the Savior's Atonement. This coal would have burned or cleansed Isaiah's sin away.

**Verses 8-10**
The last part of verse 10 could be misunderstood to say that the Lord does not want the people to be converted. Rather, this verse is saying that the people did not want to see, hear, or understand because they might be converted if they did. The first part of the verse counsels Isaiah to make the truth so clear that they cannot avoid it. The last part is referring to their attitude.

**Verses 11-13**
A teil-tree and an oak tree are both trees that cannot just be cut down. New life will shoot forth from their trunks and the tree will regenerate. So, though Israel will be "eaten" they will come forth again. "Eaten" is a term that represents the enemy coming and consuming them.

# 2 NEPHI 17

TIP In this chapter, Nephi continues to quote Isaiah. Isaiah is writing about counseling the King of Judah, King Ahaz.

**Verses 1-2**
-Ahaz is the King of Judah
-Pekah is the King of Israel (Ephraim)
- Rezin is the King of Syria
- Judah and Israel have divided from each other and set their own kings in place. Israel lives in the northern part of Israel, and Judah in the south.
- The King of Israel and the King of Syria were forming an alliance and combining forces against Assyria. Assyria was battling nations as they tried to enlarge their borders. The kings of Israel and Syria wanted King Ahaz to join with them.

**Verses 3-4**
- The Lord tells Isaiah to prophesy to Ahaz and counsel him not to join Israel and Syria, but rather to trust that the Lord will protect Judah from Assyria.
- Isaiah met King Ahaz at the springs because the king would be supervising means to protect their water supply.
- Firebrands were torches. In this case it is the tail of the kings, and their torches have gone out and are now smoking. This represented that their power was now gone.

**Verses 5-6**
Isaiah knows the plans of Syria and Israel. Their plan was to replace King Ahaz with a king of their choosing who would form the alliance with them.

**Verses 7-9**
Isaiah is prophesying of Ephraim's (Israel's) future. Judah and Israel had divided and Israel had gone north and established their own king. Isaiah knows that Israel will be taken captive, which history shows does happen. Assyria will come and deport most of the people to other countries. This is the beginning of the scattering of Israel.

**Verses 14-15**
The Lord gives Ahaz a sign and explains that his land has a great destiny to fulfill. Butter and honey were foods that children particularly liked.

**Verses 16-17**
These verses (14-16) are what is known as a dual prophecy, which Isaiah did often. He was teaching of the Savior who would be born, but also of a child born in his day (most likely his own son). This child would not be very old before Assyria would overtake their land.

**Verses 18-19**
Bees and flies symbolized soldiers coming to battle. This is referring to the ruthless Assyrian army.

**Verse 20**
War prisoners were often forced into slavery and shaven from head to toe, which was humiliating to them and their Jewish customs.

**Verses 21-23**
Those left behind shall only have a few animals and so their main diet will be milk, honey and butter.

**Verses 24-25**
Only hunters will venture into the thorns seeking meat for food.
A mattock is a hoe. These hills, which were once so cared for and cultivated, will be only left for their few grazing cattle, rather than for crops.

# 2 NEPHI 18

TIP In this chapter, Nephi continues to quote Isaiah. After King Ahaz's refusal to listen to Isaiah, Isaiah then turns to counsel the people.

**Verses 1-4**
Since Ahaz refused to heed Isaiah's counsel, Isaiah will now turn to the people and try to get them to obey the Lord.
Isaiah has two sons: Maher-sha-lal-hash-baz and Shear-jashub. Isaiah's wife, the prophetess, gives birth to Maher-sha-lal-hash-baz. This name means "to speed the spoil" which was the fate of Judah.

# 2 NEPHI 18 (CONTINUED)

**Verses 5-8**    The waters of Shiloah were gentle, flowing waters that provided life-sustaining water to the inhabitants of Jerusalem. In this context, the waters symbolized the Lord's guidance and the spiritual source for the people. Since the people are rejecting this source, another river (the Assyrians) will flood their land and gather around their necks.

**Verses 9-12**    Whenever a phrase is repeated, the message is given extra emphasis. Isaiah is warning the people against joining with Israel and Syria and combining forces against Assyria.

**Verses 13-15**    The Lord can be a protective rock of offense, or a sanctuary. But the people of Isaiah's day saw Him as a stumbling block, or as someone who was getting in their way.

**Verses 16-18**    These prophecies, now recorded, are a witness against the people.

**Verses 19-22**    These verses warn of seeking after other sources of spiritual guidance. If they do so, they will be led astray. Isaiah has recorded these words (the law and testimony), and any other forms of spiritualism will bring trouble and darkness.

# 2 NEPHI 19

> **TIP**    In this chapter, Nephi continues to quote Isaiah. Isaiah prophesies of the future Messiah and of evils that will bring destruction.

**Verse 1**    - Chapters 19 and 20 are natural continuations of chapters 17 and 18. The context centers on the threat of an Assyrian invasion.
- In 17 and 18 Isaiah warns Ahaz and the people of what would happen if they formed an alliance with Israel and Syria.
- Chapters 19 and 20 are more detailed prophecies. Since Ahaz ignored Isaiah's warnings, the alliance has now happened.
- The Land of Israel was divided as an inheritance for the descendants of the 12 tribes of Israel. Zebulun and Naphtali were given land in the northern part of Israel which bordered other nations. Their lands were known as the "Galilee of Nations" because there was a lot of mixed nationality. These lands were the first to be captured by Assyria.

**Verses 2-5**    These lands will see hard days but will yet experience greatness. The Assyrians will come and take the lands, but the Lord will ultimately devastate their armies and the land of Israel will still fulfill its destiny.

**Verses 6-7**    This is a dual prophecy. These verses speak of Christ as well as King Hezekiah. King Hezekiah was a righteous king who listened to Isaiah and tried to turn the people to the Lord.

**Verses 8-12**    - Verses 8-20 mention evils that will be destroyed and ultimately bring destruction to the people.
- These are dual prophecies. They are speaking of the destruction in Isaiah's day as well as those preceding the Second Coming.
- The people thought that they were strong enough and could replace everything that was destroyed with better things. Bricks were man-made and were inferior to hewn (carved out) stones. Cedar wood was superior to sycamore wood.

**Verses 13-17**    These verses are referencing the wicked leadership. The head is government leaders and the tail is false prophets.

**Verses 18-21**    Wickedness is compared to a forest fire that spreads everywhere using the people as fuel.

# 2 NEPHI 20

> **TIP**    In this chapter, Nephi continues to quote Isaiah. Isaiah writes about the destruction of Assyria.

**Verses 1-4**    The fourth evil from the previous chapter is in the first four verses in this chapter. Isaiah is talking about people that turn away those in need. In verse 3 he directed questions to these people. They who turned away so many, who will THEY turn to and ask for help when the destruction comes?

**Verses 5-6**    These verses prophesy of the destruction of Assyria, a nation who thought themselves to be all powerful.
The Lord calls Assyria the "rod of my anger". The Lord used Assyria to humble his people, the rod being a symbol of something that smites or strikes. If Israel and Judah would have turned to the Lord, He would have protected them from Assyria.

**Verse 7**    Assyria's intention was not to assist God but to cut down many nations for their own gain. They did not intend to further God's purposes.

**Verses 8-11**    "Are not my princes altogether kings?"
- Assyria is boasting that even their army commanders are as powerful as kings.
The King of Assyria is, again, boasting in this verse as he looked over his conquered cities. He is saying, "should I not also do this to Jerusalem?".

**Verses 12-14**    The Lord will punish Assyria who thinks that it has accomplished everything through its own power.
In verse 14, Israel is compared to a bird in its nest. The eggs in the nest represent the riches of Israel. The bird is Israel who cannot make a sound or move its wings. It is in a helpless condition with the Assyrian armies.

**Verse 15**    The ax is Assyria and the person holding the ax is the Lord. But the ax is the one taking all of the credit.

**Verses 16-19**    Assyria will be destroyed like a forest fire that destroys a forest in a single day. The thorns and briers are metaphors for wickedness and sin that provide fuel for this fire. The fire will be so complete that a child can count the trees that remain standing.

**Verses 20-22**    These verses prophesy of the gathering of Israel in the last days. Israel is gathered by being baptized into the Gospel. The House of Israel are those that are heirs of the Abrahamic Covenant and all of the promises held in that covenant. They also hold the responsibility to take the Gospel to the world.

**Verse 23**    The Lord shall "make a consumption" which means that there will be a judgment / consumption that will happen to the world. The gathered remnant of Israel have a little bit of time to gather as many of the House of Israel as possible (on both sides of the veil).

**Verses 24-26**    "My people that dwellest in Zion" is a plea for the Lord's people to trust Him, although they may be temporarily under the rule of a nation such as the Assyrians.

**Verses 27-32**    Isaiah is giving a graphic description of the Assyrians advancing armies (which is representative of wicked nations in the last days). They are getting closer and closer to Jerusalem as they pass through city after city. Isaiah does this in a way to help us feel the fear and anxiety as the situation seems more and more fearful.

**Verses 33-34**    There is sudden destruction of Assyria (or the wicked in the last days) and the righteous are spared.

# 2 NEPHI 19

LESSON LEARNED:

FAVORITE SCRIPTURE:

# 2 NEPHI 20

LESSON LEARNED:

FAVORITE SCRIPTURE:

# 2 NEPHI 21

LESSON LEARNED:

FAVORITE SCRIPTURE:

# 2 NEPHI 22

LESSON LEARNED:

FAVORITE SCRIPTURE:

# 2 NEPHI 21

**TIP** Nephi continues to quote Isaiah. Isaiah is teaching about the last days and the Millennium.

Verse 1 The "stem of Jesse" is the Mortal Messiah. Jesse was King David's father and the Messiah was prophesied to come through that kingly line which was known as the Davidic Line. Mary was a descendant of David. Some scholars suggest that the "rod" and the "branch" is Joseph Smith. This verse is a continuation of the previous chapter. The Lord will cut down the forest and replace it with a righteous tree.

Verses 2-5 These verses teach about Christ during the Millennium.

Verses 6-9 Little children will have wisdom and understanding that others can learn from. "The earth shall be full of knowledge": some scholars suggest that this teaches the desire for people to have knowledge along with the technological advancements providing that knowledge.

Verses 10-12 This verse teaches about the gathering of Israel and the Church of Jesus Christ of Latter-Day Saints standing as an Ensign to gather them.

Verses 13-14 Judah (the Southern Kingdom of Israel) and Ephraim (the Northern Kingdom of Israel) who were once divided, will now be at peace with one another. "Fly upon the shoulders of the Philistines": the Philistines in this verse mean the Gentiles. These Gentiles will invent great means for travel and communication. Verse 14 mention Israel's former enemies. In the last days, they represent any nation who stands in the way of God and His ways.

Verses 15-16 "Tongue" in verse 15 can also mean "gulf". These verses reference Moses leading the Israelites out of Egypt and across the Red Sea. This is symbolic of nations being unable to interfere with the Lord's work and the gathering of His people.

# 2 NEPHI 22

**TIP** Nephi continues to quote Isaiah. Isaiah is teaching about the last days and the Millennium.

Verses:1-6 These verses contain two short psalms. The first psalm is found in verses 1-3, and the second in verses 4-6.

# 2 NEPHI 23

**TIP** Nephi continues to quote Isaiah. Isaiah prophecies about the destruction of Babylon and the destruction at the Second Coming.

Verses 1-2 -Babylon was a symbol of the wickedness of the world. This chapter contains a dual prophecy .(the destruction of Babylon which is like the destruction of the world at the Second Coming of Jesus Christ).
- Some scholars suggest the banner (which is an Ensign) is the Book of Mormon.
- "Go into the gates": This is an invitation to enter into the Holy City (Jerusalem or New Jerusalem).

Verses 3-5 -Sanctified Ones: those that are temple worthy
- "Noise" can also be translated as "voice"
- Speaking of these verses, Joseph Smith said, "This has reference to gathering of the Saints in the Rocky Mountains." (Teachings of the Prophet Joseph Smith, 255).

Verses 6-9 -"Their faces shall be as flames": This can mean that they are experiencing intense pain or are red with shame.

Verses 10-12 -"I will make a man more precious than fine gold": so great will be the destruction that those who survive will be as fine gold.
- Ophir was a fine gold that kings would import.

Verses 13-16 A "roe" is likely a gazelle

Verses 17-19 "The Medes" were an army from Persia that had succesffully crushed Babylon.  Chaldees" is a name often used to describe Babylonians.

Verses 20-22 The fate of Babylon, or the wickedness of the world.

# 2 NEPHI 24

**TIP** Nephi continues to quote Isaiah. Isaiah prophecies about what it will be like during the Millennium.

Verses 1-3 -"Strangers shall be joined with them" refers to the uniting of the House of Israel and Gentiles in holiness.

Verses 4-8 - Verse 4 begins as a poem or song meant to be sung to the King of Babylon (who represents the head of wickedness of the world). Even the Cedars of Lebanon feel at peace since destruction has ceased.

Verses 9-11 - Satan will be bound during the Millennium. This part of the poem talks about the reaction of men and women in hell when they realize Satan is there, just as they are.

Verses 21-23 - The destruction of Babylon / the world

Verses 28-32 -Palestina was a flourishing and wealthy city that enjoyed much prosperity.
- The serpent's root, the cockatrice, and the fiery flying serpent are all symbols of evil that will ultimately come upon them.

# 2 NEPHI 25

**TIP** Nephi is no longer quoting Isaiah and is now commenting on Isaiah's writings.

# 2 NEPHI 23

LESSON LEARNED:

FAVORITE SCRIPTURE:

# 2 NEPHI 24

LESSON LEARNED:

FAVORITE SCRIPTURE:

# 2 NEPHI 25

LESSON LEARNED:

FAVORITE SCRIPTURE:

# 2 NEPHI 26

LESSON LEARNED:

FAVORITE SCRIPTURE:

# 2 NEPHI 27

LESSON LEARNED:

FAVORITE SCRIPTURE:

# 2 NEPHI 28

LESSON LEARNED:

FAVORITE SCRIPTURE:

# 2 NEPHI 29

LESSON LEARNED:

FAVORITE SCRIPTURE:

# 2 NEPHI 30

LESSON LEARNED:

FAVORITE SCRIPTURE:

# 2 NEPHI 31

LESSON LEARNED:

FAVORITE SCRIPTURE:

## 2 NEPHI 32

 LESSON LEARNED:

FAVORITE SCRIPTURE:

# 2 NEPHI 33

LESSON LEARNED:

FAVORITE SCRIPTURE:

## JACOB 1

LESSON LEARNED:

FAVORITE SCRIPTURE:

## JACOB 2

LESSON LEARNED:

FAVORITE SCRIPTURE:

## JACOB 3

LESSON LEARNED:

FAVORITE SCRIPTURE:

## JACOB 4

LESSON LEARNED:

FAVORITE SCRIPTURE:

## JACOB 5

LESSON LEARNED:
* Study Jacob 5 using the illustrations on pages 34-35 before filling in this box.

FAVORITE SCRIPTURE:

# THE ALLEGORY OF THE OLIVE TREE / JACOB 5

**Tip**

Jacob had studied the words of the prophets on the brass plates. On those plates there were the writings of the prophet Zenos whose record we no longer have. While Jacob was teaching the people, he quoted "The Allegory of the Tame and Wild Olive Trees" which Zenos had originally recorded.

As you study Jacob 5, follow along the boxes below. As you study doodle notes, details, pictures, questions, etc.

**First Visit / Verses 1-14**

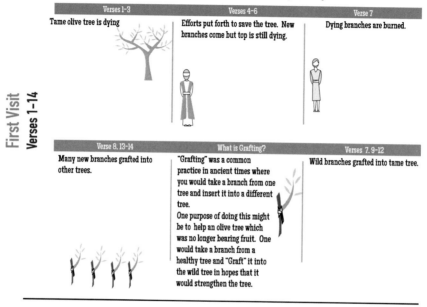

| Verses 1-3 | Verses 4-6 | Verse 7 |
|---|---|---|
| Tame olive tree is dying | Efforts put forth to save the tree. New branches come but top is still dying. | Dying branches are burned. |

| Verse 8, 13-14 | What is Grafting? | Verses 7, 9-12 |
|---|---|---|
| Many new branches grafted into other trees. | "Grafting" was a common practice in ancient times where you would take a branch from one tree and insert it into a different tree. One purpose of doing this might be to help an olive tree which was no longer bearing fruit. One would take a branch from a healthy tree and "Graft" it into the wild tree in hopes that it would strengthen the tree. | Wild branches grafted into tame tree. |

**Second Visit / Verses 15-28**

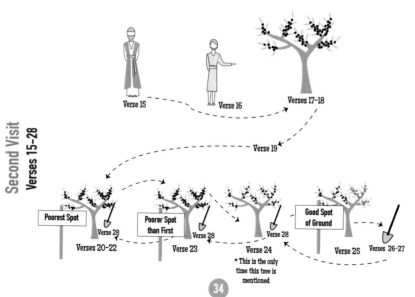

Verse 15

Verse 16

Verses 17-18

Verse 19

Poorest Spot — Verse 28 — Verses 20-22

Poorer Spot than First — Verse 28 — Verse 23

Verse 28 — Verse 24
* This is the only time this tree is mentioned

Good Spot of Ground — Verse 25 — Verses 26-27

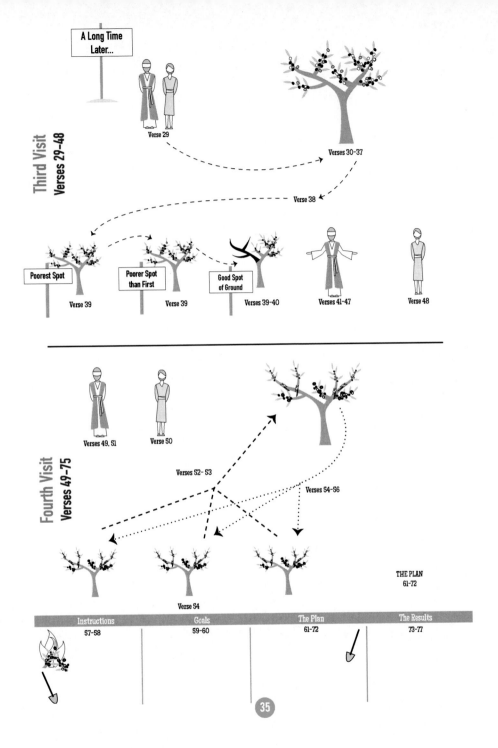

**Third Visit**
**Verses 29–48**

A Long Time Later...

Verse 29

Verses 30-37

Verse 38

Poorest Spot
Verse 39

Poorer Spot than First
Verse 39

Good Spot of Ground
Verses 39-40

Verses 41-47

Verse 48

**Fourth Visit**
**Verses 49–75**

Verses 49, 51

Verse 50

Verses 52- 53

Verses 54-56

Verse 54

THE PLAN
61-72

| Instructions | Goals | The Plan | The Results |
|---|---|---|---|
| 57-58 | 59-60 | 61-72 | 73-77 |

## JACOB 6

LESSON LEARNED:

FAVORITE SCRIPTURE:

## JACOB 7

LESSON LEARNED:

FAVORITE SCRIPTURE:

## ENOS 1

LESSON LEARNED:

FAVORITE SCRIPTURE:

LESSON LEARNED:

## JAROM 1

FAVORITE SCRIPTURE:

# UNDERSTANDING WHO THE NEPHITES WERE

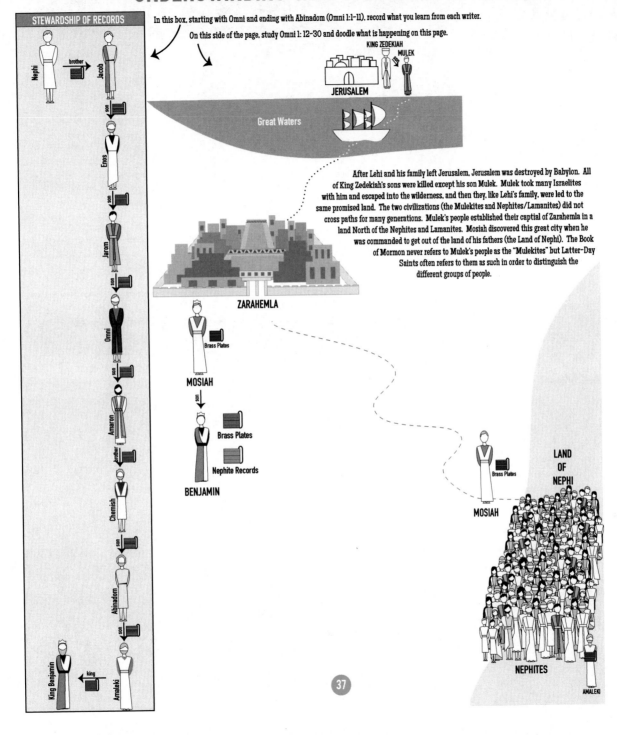

**STEWARDSHIP OF RECORDS**

In this box, starting with Omni and ending with Abinadom (Omni 1:1-11), record what you learn from each writer.

On this side of the page, study Omni 1: 12-30 and doodle what is happening on this page.

Nephi → brother → Jacob

Enos — son

Jarom — son

Omni — son

Amaron — son

Chemish — brother

Abinadom — son

Amaleki — king → King Benjamin

**KING ZEDEKIAH**
**MULEK**
**JERUSALEM**

Great Waters

After Lehi and his family left Jerusalem, Jerusalem was destroyed by Babylon. All of King Zedekiah's sons were killed except his son Mulek. Mulek took many Israelites with him and escaped into the wilderness, and then they, like Lehi's family, were led to the same promised land. The two civilizations (the Mulekites and Nephites/Lamanites) did not cross paths for many generations. Mulek's people established their captial of Zarahemla in a land North of the Nephites and Lamanites. Mosiah discovered this great city when he was commanded to get out of the land of his fathers (the Land of Nephi). The Book of Mormon never refers to Mulek's people as the "Mulekites" but Latter-Day Saints often refers to them as such in order to distinguish the different groups of people.

**ZARAHEMLA**

Brass Plates

**MOSIAH**

son

Brass Plates

Nephite Records

**BENJAMIN**

Brass Plates

**MOSIAH**

**LAND OF NEPHI**

**NEPHITES**

**AMALEKI**

# OMNI 1

**LESSON LEARNED:**

*Study Omni 1 using the illustrations on page 37 before filling in this box.

**FAVORITE SCRIPTURE:**

# WORDS OF MORMON 1

**LESSON LEARNED:**

**FAVORITE SCRIPTURE:**

# MOSIAH 1

**LESSON LEARNED:**

**FAVORITE SCRIPTURE:**

# MOSIAH 2

**LESSON LEARNED:**

**FAVORITE SCRIPTURE:**

## MOSIAH 3

LESSON LEARNED:

FAVORITE SCRIPTURE:

## MOSIAH 4

LESSON LEARNED:

FAVORITE SCRIPTURE:

## MOSIAH 5

LESSON LEARNED:

FAVORITE SCRIPTURE:

## MOSIAH 6

LESSON LEARNED:

FAVORITE SCRIPTURE:

# UNDERSTANDING THE TIMELINE IN MOSIAH / MOSIAH 7

**Tip**

The Book of Mosiah can be confusing because it jumps back and forth to different time periods. Years before this point in King Mosiah II's life (2 generations before him), there was a group of Nephites who had left Zarahemla with the hopes of regaining the land of their fathers (the Land of Nephi). A man named Zeniff led them. That group of Nephites had not been heard of since; and King Mosiah II was concerned with their whereabouts and well-being, so he sent a search party to find them. Mosiah 7-8 is the journey of this group finding those lost Nephites. Mosiah 9-24 is the story of the Lost Nephites and what had happened once they left Zarahemla.

Read verses 1-8 and write what is happening on each part of this picture.

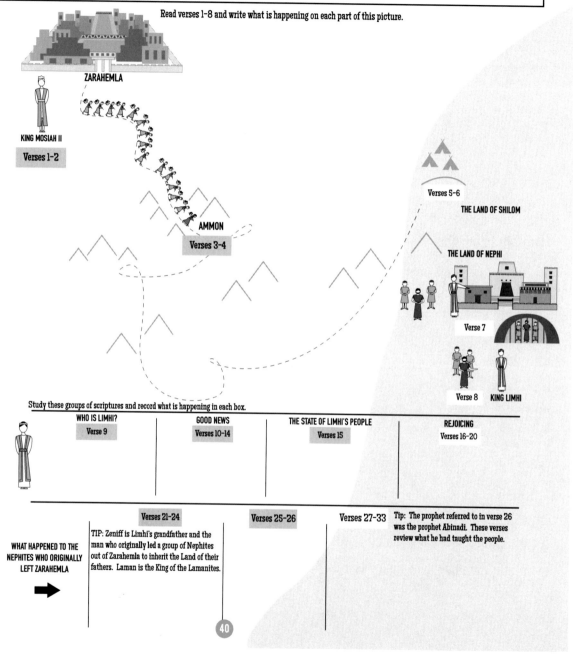

ZARAHEMLA

KING MOSIAH II

Verses 1-2

AMMON

Verses 3-4

Verses 5-6

THE LAND OF SHILOM

THE LAND OF NEPHI

Verse 7

Verse 8    KING LIMHI

Study these groups of scriptures and record what is happening in each box.

| WHO IS LIMHI? Verse 9 | GOOD NEWS Verses 10-14 | THE STATE OF LIMHI'S PEOPLE Verse 15 | REJOICING Verses 16-20 |
|---|---|---|---|
| | | | |

| WHAT HAPPENED TO THE NEPHITES WHO ORIGINALLY LEFT ZARAHEMLA → | Verses 21-24 TIP: Zeniff is Limhi's grandfather and the man who originally led a group of Nephites out of Zarahemla to inherit the Land of their fathers. Laman is the King of the Lamanites. | Verses 25-26 | Verses 27-33  Tip: The prophet referred to in verse 26 was the prophet Abinadi. These verses review what he had taught the people. |

## MOSIAH 7

## MOSIAH 8

**LESSON LEARNED:**

*Study Mosiah 7-8 using the illustrations on page 40 before filling in these boxes.

**LESSON LEARNED:**

**FAVORITE SCRIPTURE:**

**FAVORITE SCRIPTURE:**

## MOSIAH 9

## MOSIAH 10

**LESSON LEARNED:**

**LESSON LEARNED:**

**FAVORITE SCRIPTURE:**

**FAVORITE SCRIPTURE:**

# MOSIAH 11

LESSON LEARNED:

FAVORITE SCRIPTURE:

# MOSIAH 12

LESSON LEARNED:

FAVORITE SCRIPTURE:

# MOSIAH 13

LESSON LEARNED:

FAVORITE SCRIPTURE:

# MOSIAH 14

LESSON LEARNED:
*Use the Isaiah tips on the following page to help you understand this chapter.

FAVORITE SCRIPTURE:

# MOSIAH 14

TIP

In the midst of Abinadi's teachings, he quotes Isaiah. This particular prophecy of Isaiah is called a "Messianic Prophecy" which means it is a prophecy that teaches about the Messiah who will come and save all men. Abinadi quotes Isaiah in chapter 14 and then gives commentary on it in chapter 15.

Considering what Abinadi was teaching in the last chapter (Mosiah 13), why do you think he quoted a "Messianic Prophecy" from the prophet Isaiah, whom the council itself had just quoted in Mosiah 12:21-24?

14:1    There are 2 questions in this verse that precede the verses that teach about a God coming to earth to be a mortal.

14:2    - A tender plant is a young and vulnerable plant, like an innocent child. It is also not a grand plant that others may take notice of, like a king or person of great importance.
- A plant does not usually take root in dry ground. The Jewish religion in his day was "dry". While there were many faithful Jews, the leadership had become corrupt.
- This verse does not necessarily suggest that Christ was unattractive, but that He did not stand out in a physical way.

14:3-5  - Verse 3 prophecies of Christ's life and things He will face.
- The word "borne" can also be translated as "forgiven".

14:6    - When a sheep strays from his flock, he has no sense of where he is and must be brought back by another source.

14:7-8  "Who shall declare his generation" refers to the Jewish tradition that one year after a father's death his son will "declare his generation," meaning that he will continue his father's seed. The son promises to carry on his father's legacy, family, and purpose.

14:9-12 "It pleased the Lord" can also be translated, "it was the will of the Lord".

# MOSIAH 15

LESSON LEARNED:

FAVORITE SCRIPTURE:

# MOSIAH 16

LESSON LEARNED:

FAVORITE SCRIPTURE:

# MOSIAH 17

LESSON LEARNED:

FAVORITE SCRIPTURE:

# MOSIAH 18

LESSON LEARNED:

FAVORITE SCRIPTURE:

# MOSIAH 19

**LESSON LEARNED:**

**FAVORITE SCRIPTURE:**

# MOSIAH 20

**LESSON LEARNED:**

**FAVORITE SCRIPTURE:**

# MOSIAH 21

**LESSON LEARNED:**

**FAVORITE SCRIPTURE:**

# MOSIAH 22

**LESSON LEARNED:**

**FAVORITE SCRIPTURE:**

# MOSIAH 23

**LESSON LEARNED:**

**FAVORITE SCRIPTURE:**

# MOSIAH 24

**LESSON LEARNED:**

**FAVORITE SCRIPTURE:**

# MOSIAH 25

**LESSON LEARNED:**

**FAVORITE SCRIPTURE:**

# MOSIAH 26

**LESSON LEARNED:**

**FAVORITE SCRIPTURE:**

# MOSIAH 27

LESSON LEARNED:

FAVORITE SCRIPTURE:

# MOSIAH 28

LESSON LEARNED:

FAVORITE SCRIPTURE:

# MOSIAH 29

LESSON LEARNED:

FAVORITE SCRIPTURE:

LESSON LEARNED:

ALMA
1

FAVORITE SCRIPTURE:

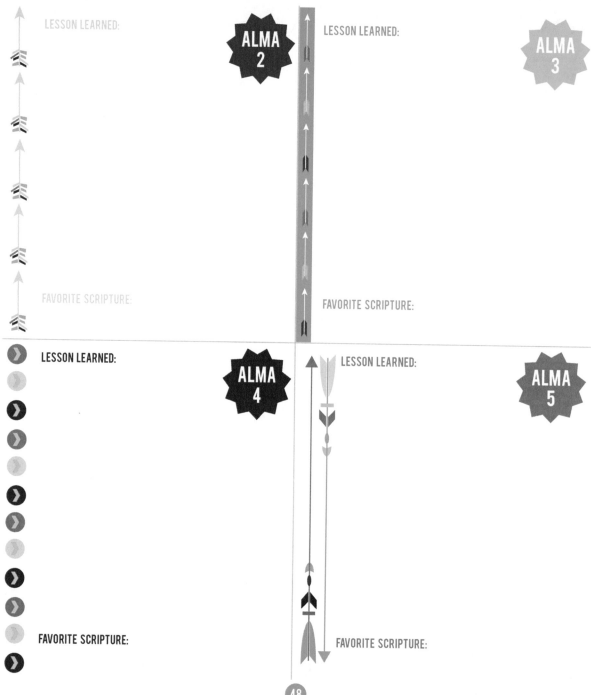

LESSON LEARNED:

ALMA
2

LESSON LEARNED:

ALMA
3

FAVORITE SCRIPTURE:

FAVORITE SCRIPTURE:

LESSON LEARNED:

ALMA
4

LESSON LEARNED:

ALMA
5

FAVORITE SCRIPTURE:

FAVORITE SCRIPTURE:

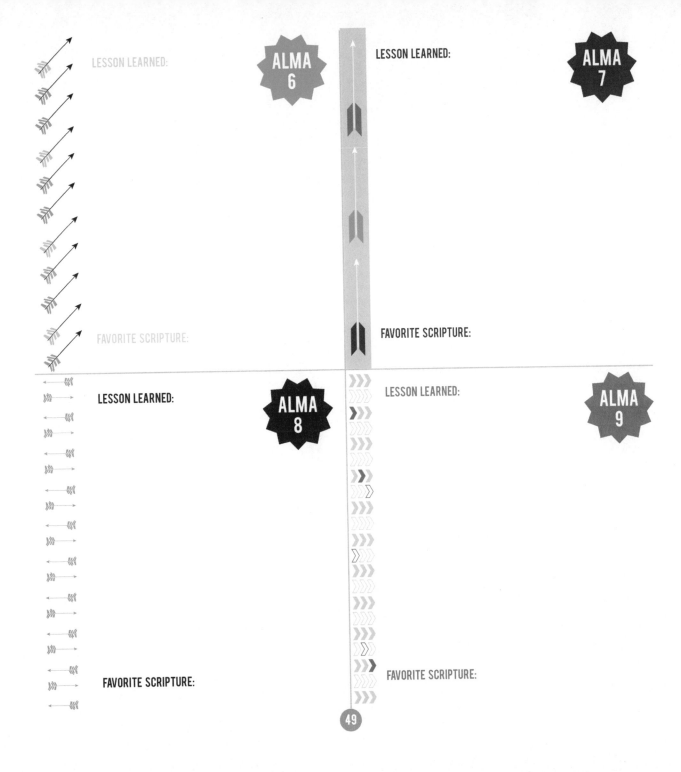

LESSON LEARNED:

ALMA
6

LESSON LEARNED:

ALMA
7

FAVORITE SCRIPTURE:

FAVORITE SCRIPTURE:

LESSON LEARNED:

ALMA
8

LESSON LEARNED:

ALMA
9

FAVORITE SCRIPTURE:

FAVORITE SCRIPTURE:

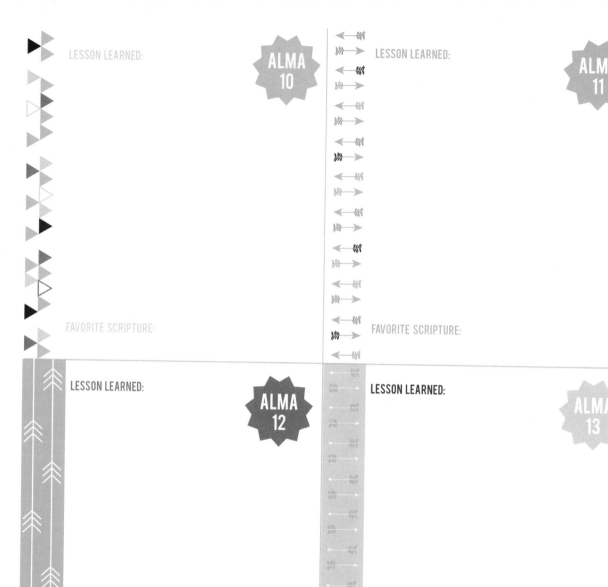

LESSON LEARNED:

**ALMA 10**

LESSON LEARNED:

**ALMA 11**

FAVORITE SCRIPTURE:

FAVORITE SCRIPTURE:

LESSON LEARNED:

**ALMA 12**

LESSON LEARNED:

**ALMA 13**

FAVORITE SCRIPTURE:

FAVORITE SCRIPTURE:

LESSON LEARNED:

ALMA
14

LESSON LEARNED:

ALMA
15

FAVORITE SCRIPTURE:

FAVORITE SCRIPTURE:

LESSON LEARNED:

ALMA
16

LESSON LEARNED:

ALMA
17

FAVORITE SCRIPTURE:

FAVORITE SCRIPTURE:

51

LESSON LEARNED:

ALMA
18

LESSON LEARNED:

ALMA
19

FAVORITE SCRIPTURE:

FAVORITE SCRIPTURE:

LESSON LEARNED:

ALMA
20

LESSON LEARNED:

ALMA
21

FAVORITE SCRIPTURE:

FAVORITE SCRIPTURE:

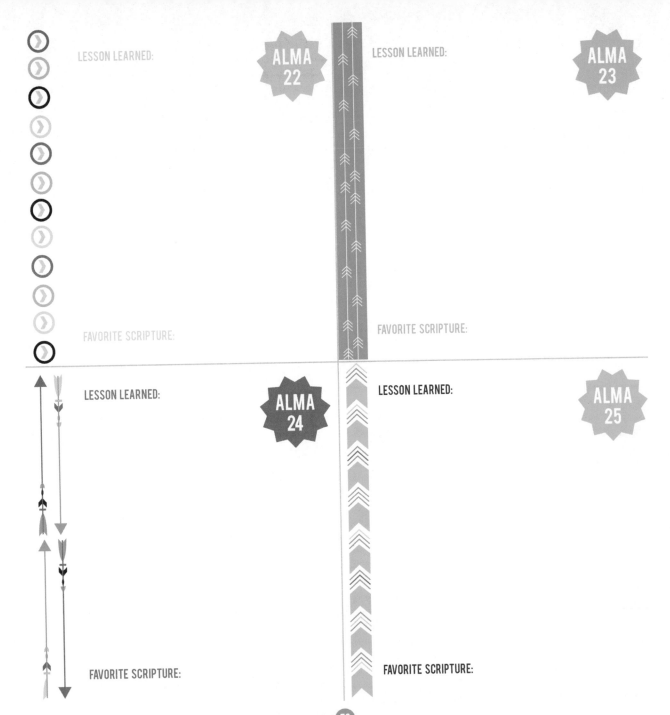

LESSON LEARNED:

**ALMA 22**

LESSON LEARNED:

**ALMA 23**

FAVORITE SCRIPTURE:

FAVORITE SCRIPTURE:

LESSON LEARNED:

**ALMA 24**

LESSON LEARNED:

**ALMA 25**

FAVORITE SCRIPTURE:

FAVORITE SCRIPTURE:

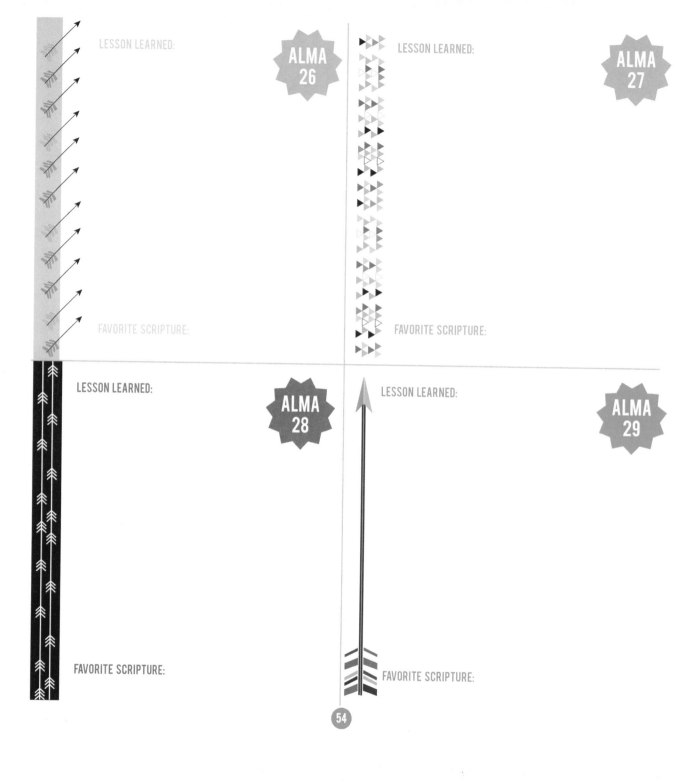

LESSON LEARNED:

ALMA
26

FAVORITE SCRIPTURE:

LESSON LEARNED:

ALMA
27

FAVORITE SCRIPTURE:

LESSON LEARNED:

ALMA
28

FAVORITE SCRIPTURE:

LESSON LEARNED:

ALMA
29

FAVORITE SCRIPTURE:

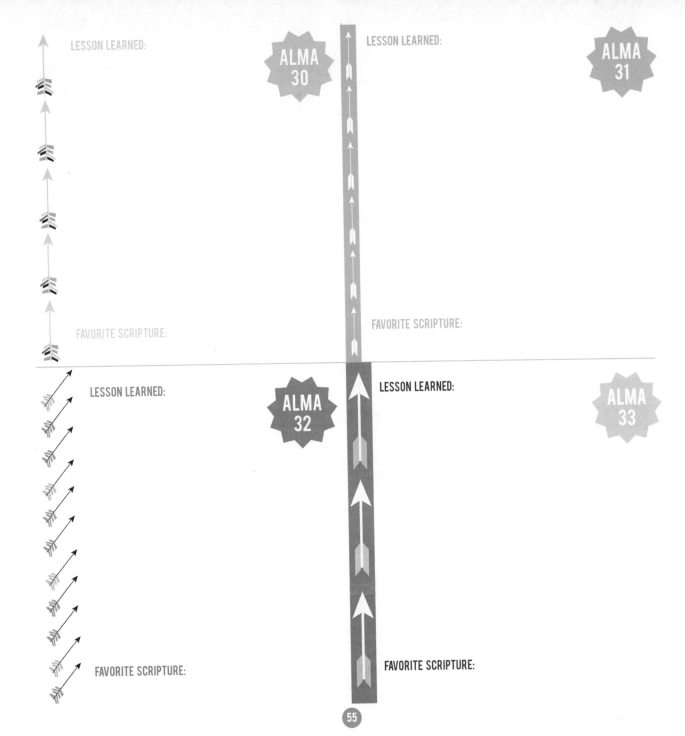

LESSON LEARNED:

LESSON LEARNED:

ALMA
30

ALMA
31

FAVORITE SCRIPTURE:

FAVORITE SCRIPTURE:

LESSON LEARNED:

LESSON LEARNED:

ALMA
32

ALMA
33

FAVORITE SCRIPTURE:

FAVORITE SCRIPTURE:

55

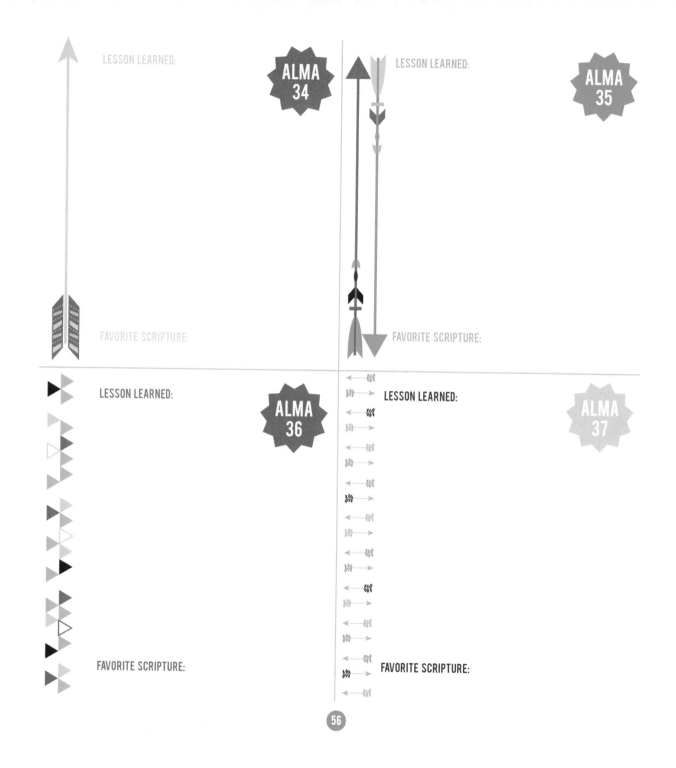

LESSON LEARNED:

ALMA
34

LESSON LEARNED:

ALMA
35

FAVORITE SCRIPTURE:

FAVORITE SCRIPTURE:

LESSON LEARNED:

ALMA
36

LESSON LEARNED:

ALMA
37

FAVORITE SCRIPTURE:

FAVORITE SCRIPTURE:

LESSON LEARNED:

ALMA
38

FAVORITE SCRIPTURE:

LESSON LEARNED:

ALMA
39

FAVORITE SCRIPTURE:

LESSON LEARNED:

ALMA
40

FAVORITE SCRIPTURE:

LESSON LEARNED:

ALMA
41

FAVORITE SCRIPTURE:

LESSON LEARNED:

ALMA
42

LESSON LEARNED:

ALMA
43

FAVORITE SCRIPTURE:

FAVORITE SCRIPTURE:

LESSON LEARNED:

ALMA
44

LESSON LEARNED:

ALMA
45

FAVORITE SCRIPTURE:

FAVORITE SCRIPTURE:

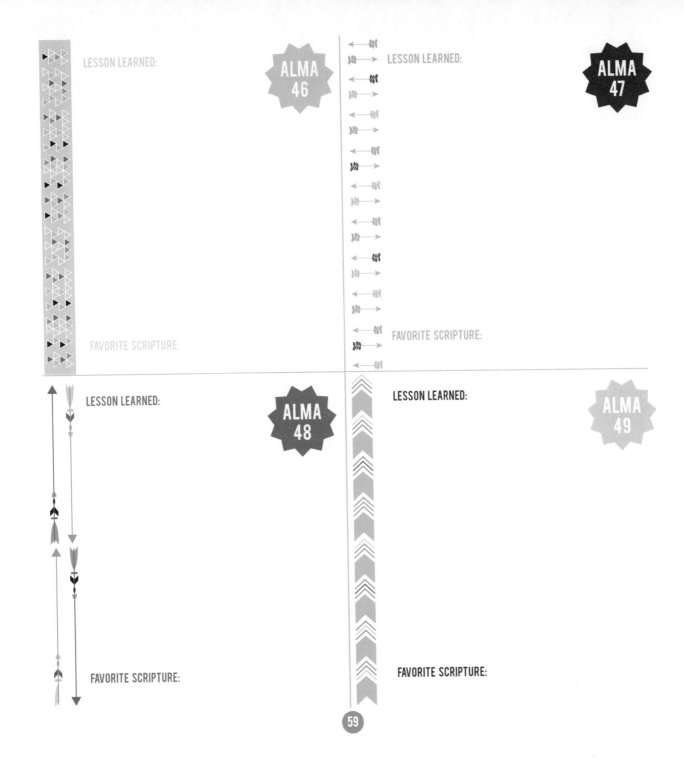

LESSON LEARNED:

ALMA
46

FAVORITE SCRIPTURE:

LESSON LEARNED:

ALMA
47

FAVORITE SCRIPTURE:

LESSON LEARNED:

ALMA
48

FAVORITE SCRIPTURE:

LESSON LEARNED:

ALMA
49

FAVORITE SCRIPTURE:

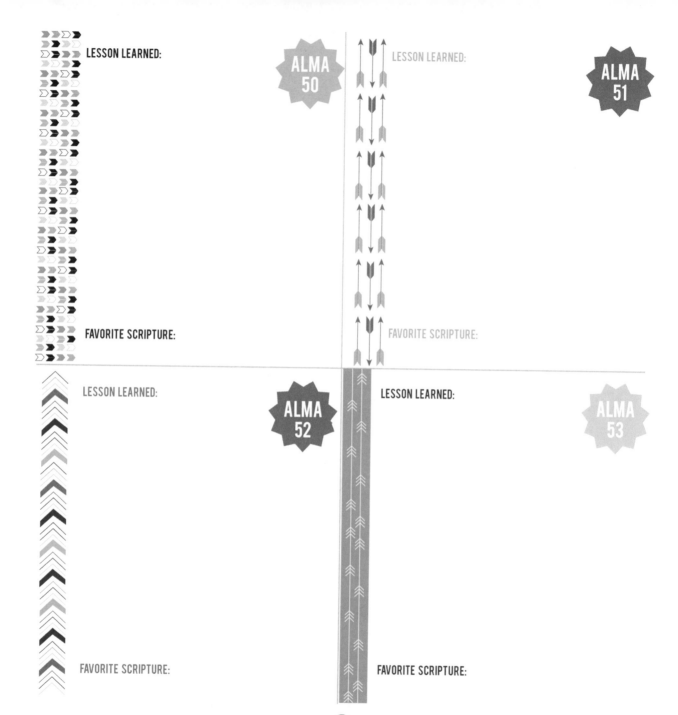

**LESSON LEARNED:**

ALMA
50

**FAVORITE SCRIPTURE:**

**LESSON LEARNED:**

ALMA
51

**FAVORITE SCRIPTURE:**

**LESSON LEARNED:**

ALMA
52

**FAVORITE SCRIPTURE:**

**LESSON LEARNED:**

ALMA
53

**FAVORITE SCRIPTURE:**

LESSON LEARNED:

ALMA
54

LESSON LEARNED:

ALMA
55

FAVORITE SCRIPTURE:

FAVORITE SCRIPTURE:

LESSON LEARNED:

ALMA
56

LESSON LEARNED:

ALMA
57

FAVORITE SCRIPTURE:

FAVORITE SCRIPTURE:

LESSON LEARNED:

**ALMA 58**

LESSON LEARNED:

**ALMA 59**

FAVORITE SCRIPTURE:

FAVORITE SCRIPTURE:

LESSON LEARNED:

**ALMA 60**

LESSON LEARNED:

**ALMA 61**

FAVORITE SCRIPTURE:

FAVORITE SCRIPTURE:

ALMA
62

ALMA
63

FAVORITE SCRIPTURE:

FAVORITE SCRIPTURE:

# HELAMAN 1

# HELAMAN 2

LESSON LEARNED:

**LESSON LEARNED:**

FAVORITE SCRIPTURE:

**FAVORITE SCRIPTURE:**

# HELAMAN 3

LESSON LEARNED:

FAVORITE SCRIPTURE:

# HELAMAN 4

LESSON LEARNED:

FAVORITE SCRIPTURE:

# HELAMAN 5

LESSON LEARNED:

FAVORITE SCRIPTURE:

# HELAMAN 6

LESSON LEARNED:

FAVORITE SCRIPTURE:

# HELAMAN 7

LESSON LEARNED:

FAVORITE SCRIPTURE:

# HELAMAN 8

LESSON LEARNED:

FAVORITE SCRIPTURE:

# HELAMAN 9

LESSON LEARNED:

FAVORITE SCRIPTURE:

# HELAMAN 10

LESSON LEARNED:

FAVORITE SCRIPTURE:

# HELAMAN 11

LESSON LEARNED:

FAVORITE SCRIPTURE:

# HELAMAN 12

LESSON LEARNED:

FAVORITE SCRIPTURE:

# HELAMAN 13

LESSON LEARNED:

FAVORITE SCRIPTURE:

# HELAMAN 14

LESSON LEARNED:

FAVORITE SCRIPTURE:

# HELAMAN 15

LESSON LEARNED:

FAVORITE SCRIPTURE:

# HELAMAN 16

FAVORITE SCRIPTURE:

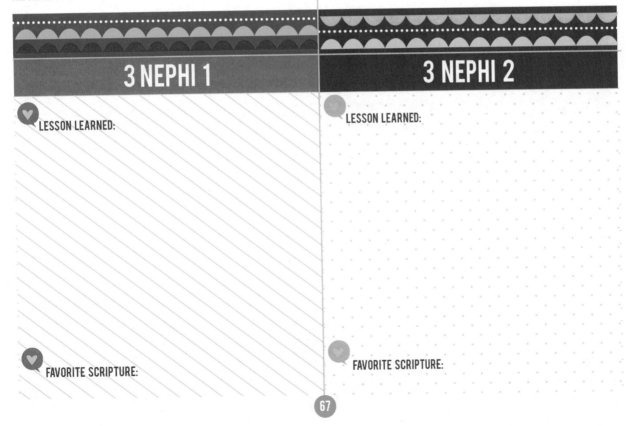

## 3 NEPHI 1

LESSON LEARNED:

FAVORITE SCRIPTURE:

## 3 NEPHI 2

LESSON LEARNED:

FAVORITE SCRIPTURE:

## 3 NEPHI 3

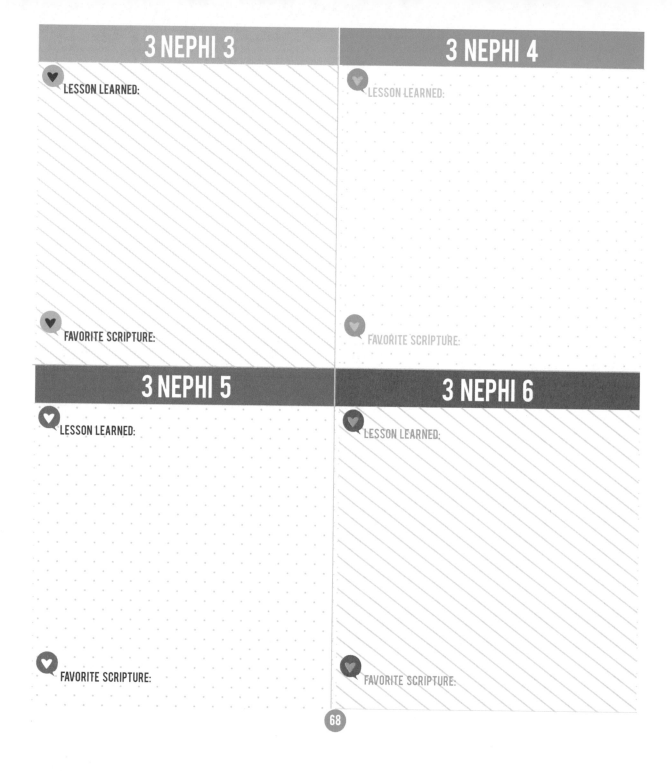

LESSON LEARNED:

FAVORITE SCRIPTURE:

## 3 NEPHI 4

LESSON LEARNED:

FAVORITE SCRIPTURE:

## 3 NEPHI 5

LESSON LEARNED:

FAVORITE SCRIPTURE:

## 3 NEPHI 6

LESSON LEARNED:

FAVORITE SCRIPTURE:

## 3 NEPHI 7

LESSON LEARNED:

FAVORITE SCRIPTURE:

## 3 NEPHI 8

LESSON LEARNED:

FAVORITE SCRIPTURE:

## 3 NEPHI 9

LESSON LEARNED:

FAVORITE SCRIPTURE:

## 3 NEPHI 10

LESSON LEARNED:

FAVORITE SCRIPTURE:

## 3 NEPHI 11

LESSON LEARNED:

FAVORITE SCRIPTURE:

## 3 NEPHI 12

LESSON LEARNED:

FAVORITE SCRIPTURE:

## 3 NEPHI 13

LESSON LEARNED:

FAVORITE SCRIPTURE:

## 3 NEPHI 14

LESSON LEARNED:

FAVORITE SCRIPTURE:

# 3 NEPHI 15

♥ **LESSON LEARNED:**

♥ **FAVORITE SCRIPTURE:**

# 3 NEPHI 16

♥ LESSON LEARNED:

♥ FAVORITE SCRIPTURE:

# 3 NEPHI 17

● LESSON LEARNED:

● FAVORITE SCRIPTURE:

# 3 NEPHI 18

♥ **LESSON LEARNED:**

♥ **FAVORITE SCRIPTURE:**

## 3 NEPHI 19

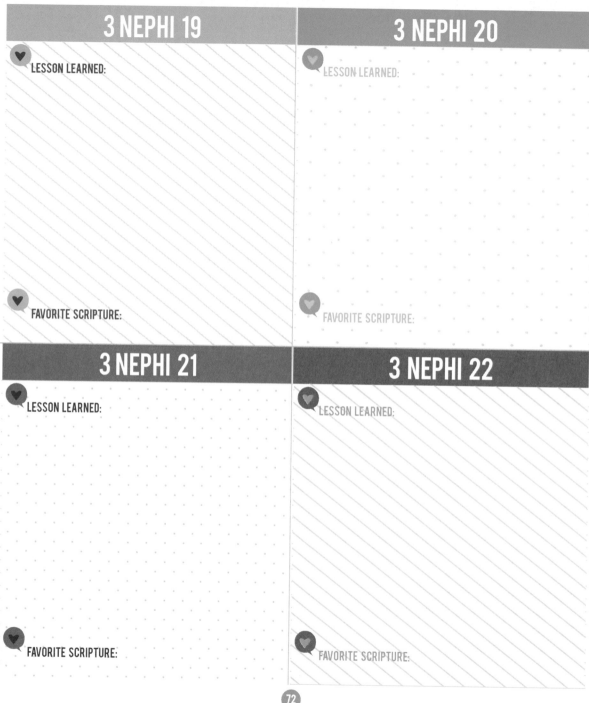

LESSON LEARNED:

FAVORITE SCRIPTURE:

## 3 NEPHI 20

LESSON LEARNED:

FAVORITE SCRIPTURE:

## 3 NEPHI 21

LESSON LEARNED:

FAVORITE SCRIPTURE:

## 3 NEPHI 22

LESSON LEARNED:

FAVORITE SCRIPTURE:

## 3 NEPHI 23

LESSON LEARNED:

FAVORITE SCRIPTURE:

## 3 NEPHI 24

LESSON LEARNED:

FAVORITE SCRIPTURE:

## 3 NEPHI 25

LESSON LEARNED:

FAVORITE SCRIPTURE:

## 3 NEPHI 26

LESSON LEARNED:

FAVORITE SCRIPTURE:

## 3 NEPHI 27

LESSON LEARNED:

FAVORITE SCRIPTURE:

## 3 NEPHI 28

LESSON LEARNED:

FAVORITE SCRIPTURE:

## 3 NEPHI 29

LESSON LEARNED:

FAVORITE SCRIPTURE:

## 3 NEPHI 30

LESSON LEARNED:

FAVORITE SCRIPTURE:

# 4 NEPHI 1

LESSON LEARNED:

FAVORITE SCRIPTURE:

MORMON 1

LESSON LEARNED:

FAVORITE SCRIPTURE:

MORMON 2

LESSON LEARNED:

FAVORITE SCRIPTURE:

MORMON 3

LESSON LEARNED:

FAVORITE SCRIPTURE:

MORMON 4

LESSON LEARNED:

FAVORITE SCRIPTURE:

MORMON 5

LESSON LEARNED:

FAVORITE SCRIPTURE:

MORMON 6

LESSON LEARNED:

FAVORITE SCRIPTURE:

MORMON 7

LESSON LEARNED:

FAVORITE SCRIPTURE:

## MORMON 8

**LESSON LEARNED:**

**FAVORITE SCRIPTURE:**

## MORMON 9

**LESSON LEARNED:**

**FAVORITE SCRIPTURE:**

## ETHER 1

**LESSON LEARNED:**

**FAVORITE SCRIPTURE:**

## ETHER 2

**LESSON LEARNED:**

**FAVORITE SCRIPTURE:**

# ETHER 3

**LESSON LEARNED:**

**FAVORITE SCRIPTURE:**

# ETHER 4

**LESSON LEARNED:**

**FAVORITE SCRIPTURE:**

# ETHER 5

**LESSON LEARNED:**

**FAVORITE SCRIPTURE:**

# ETHER 6

**LESSON LEARNED:**

**FAVORITE SCRIPTURE:**

# ETHER 7

LESSON LEARNED:

FAVORITE SCRIPTURE:

# ETHER 8

LESSON LEARNED:

FAVORITE SCRIPTURE:

# ETHER 9

LESSON LEARNED:

FAVORITE SCRIPTURE:

# ETHER 10

LESSON LEARNED:

FAVORITE SCRIPTURE:

# ETHER 11

**LESSON LEARNED:**

**FAVORITE SCRIPTURE:**

# ETHER 12

**LESSON LEARNED:**

**FAVORITE SCRIPTURE:**

# ETHER 13

**LESSON LEARNED:**

**FAVORITE SCRIPTURE:**

# ETHER 14

**LESSON LEARNED:**

**FAVORITE SCRIPTURE:**

# ETHER 15

LESSON LEARNED:

FAVORITE SCRIPTURE:

## MORONI 1

LESSON LEARNED:

FAVORITE SCRIPTURE:

## MORONI 2

LESSON LEARNED:

FAVORITE SCRIPTURE:

## MORONI 3

LESSON LEARNED:

FAVORITE SCRIPTURE:

## MORONI 4

**LESSON LEARNED:**

**FAVORITE SCRIPTURE:**

## MORONI 5

**LESSON LEARNED:**

**FAVORITE SCRIPTURE:**

## MORONI 6

**LESSON LEARNED:**

**FAVORITE SCRIPTURE:**

## MORONI 7

**LESSON LEARNED:**

**FAVORITE SCRIPTURE:**

## MORONI 8

**LESSON LEARNED:**

**FAVORITE SCRIPTURE:**

## MORONI 9

**LESSON LEARNED:**

**FAVORITE SCRIPTURE:**

## MORONI 10

**LESSON LEARNED:**

**FAVORITE SCRIPTURE:**

Made in the USA
San Bernardino, CA
06 January 2016